The Strategy of FX Risk Management in International Trade

| Author's introduction |

Dr. Jay Eom

Adjunct professor/Ph.D.

He earned a bachelor's degree at Korea University. And he received a PhD degree at Seoul School of Integrated Sciences and Technologies. He is managing 'The Institute for Business Platform'. And he is working for Donaldson Korea as the Finance Head. He had worked for Eland group and Toshiba Electronics Korea He wrote the below papers.

"Exploratory study on causality of foreign exchange exposure and hedge strategy : Systems thinking approach" Korea System Dynamics Review, 15(2), 97-131.

"Platform Strategy of Eland China for the Business Ecosystem in Emerging market: On the base of Cross-type Architecture Model from SPICE and CPNT" Korean Management Consulting Review, 14(4), 201-212

"A System Dynamics Simulation on KIKO Derivatives and its Implications from International Trade" Korea System Dynamics Review, 15(4), 5-24.

** This Book was written on the basis of the dissertation for the Ph.D. in Seoul School of Integrated Sciences & Technologies*

Abstract

According to the exchange rate, companies may be faced on the risk of financial loss. The financial loss caused by the fluctuation of exchange rate has significant impact to the company value on the short and long-term. Sometimes, it makes effect to the success or failure of a company. During the Asian financial crisis in 1997 and the global financial crisis in 2008, many Korean companies went bankrupt due to drastic fluctuation of exchange rate. It is not easy to explain the changes in the enterprise value caused by foreign currency exposure in a linear approach. This study will take a systematic approach to the causal relationship between the foreign exchange exposure and the strategy to alleviate the exposure, and provide the explanation through simulations. In addition, this study aims to confirm through empirical analysis that the causal relations are statistically meaningful.

This book is a combination of multiple studies prepared and published as separate papers. Chapter 1 explains the background, needs, and purpose, etc. of the study. Chapter 2 shows theoretical background of foreign exchange exposure and FX risk management strategy, and theoretical background of system dynamics. Chapter 3 introduces various maps, which are made on the base of documents on foreign exchange exposure published at home and abroad, and takes an approach on the system dynamics structure. Through the causal loop diagram, this book analyzed the facts that the various structures of companies had different impact on the level of foreign exchange exposure, and, as a result, hedging strategy should be different. Chapter 4 explains the impact from the derivatives selected by the company as part of its strategy to hedge against the foreign currency exposure. In particular, this book carried out the simulation of dynamics simulation from serious problem that could be occurred because the company overlooked the risk of the KIKO(Knock-In, Knock-Out) derivatives. This book tries to carry out a simulation through summarizing the problem based on the stock-and-flow structure. In chapter 5, this book analyzed the impacts from the exchange rate fluctuation to the elements of the financial statement, with the manufacturing (non-financial) companies that were traded in KOSPI and KOSDAQ. This empirical study supports the causal loop diagram and simulation on system dynamics. Lastly, chapter 6 concludes the study through discovering overall lessons and meanings.

Table of Contents

List of Tables

List of Figures

I Introduction

With the industry getting more complicated, and networking more active, the era that the company-to-company, company-to-customer, and customer-to-customer exchange take place has begun. Companies are getting involved in each other's value chain through mutual exchange, and building their eco-system (Moore, 1993). In particular, companies have transactions beyond the geological boundaries, and the exchange rate has become an important issue in the transactions between countries. It is getting more difficult to understand the complex economic system through a simple, linear approach. In this global business eco-system, the impact of exchange rate on businesses should be recognized and approached in a complex manner, instead of through a simple approach. Therefore, it is meaningful to try to understand the impact from the exchange rate through system dynamics. Although it is not easy to carry out studies through system dynamics, it provides convincing explanation to complex phenomena. Companies consider the exchange rate as a matter that cannot be controlled. However, instead of considering the change in exchange rate as a crisis that suddenly comes to the companies, if they understand the structure and respond appropriately, the changes in the exchange rate may turn into a good opportunity to companies. This book will explain various impacts of the exchange rate to the companies and the adequate responses to them. The foreign currency exposure may be determined as the sensitivity of the enterprise value to the unexpected fluctuation in exchange rate (Adler and Dumas, 1984a). Since foreign currency exposure has risks deriving from the company's structure, the exchange rate risk should be understood as a problem related to the company's structure. Therefore, this book tried to verify it with empirical study, after the analysis on the problem of the structure of corporation with system dynamics. Through this research, the study of foreign exchange can be more diverse, and companies can be easy to approach the problems caused by foreign exchange risk.

This book has been studied with the system dynamics and the empirical study. System Dynamics and the statistical method are different on philosophical background. Statistical method is suitable for the short terms on study, but system dynamics try to explain a feedback structure that does not show the visible symptoms (Kim, Moon, & Kim, 1999). It is not simple that we handle out the both method, together. This is because each has the different philosophical view, and it might lead to some confusion. I had considered the kind of confusion. But I believes that it will make valuables in system dynamics from what the statistical method is dealt with in this study.

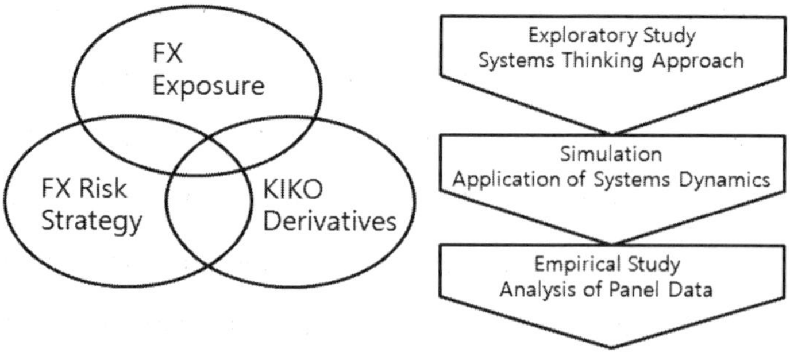

<Figure 1> The Structure of this Study

This book, when looked in large, is composed as shown in <Figure 1>. This book contains the foreign exchange exposure, the foreign exchange risk management strategy, and derivatives. Features of these contents have an important relationship with the exchange rate fluctuation. It is because the exchange risk of the company increases depending on the exchange rate fluctuation, thereby becoming to find appropriate exchange risk management strategy.

In the book, as the study methods, it tries exploratory research using the causal maps and simulation method of system dynamics. Through this, while the study is away from at single-linear method depending on the exchange rate fluctuation, it analyzes using causal map and simulation of system dynamics. In addition, through a panel analysis, it is supporting that the system dynamics analysis of this book is useful. Specifically looking at each Chapter, they are as follows.

In Chapter 1, it introduces an overall summary of this study. Through this, the reader can see an overview of the study.

In Chapter 2, it shows theoretical backgrounds of this study. Depending on the contents, it describes the theoretical backgrounds for the foreign exchange exposure and exchange risk management strategy by exchange rate fluctuation in the financial sector of the company. Since the important study method of this book is coming from system dynamics theory, and it has also described the theoretical background of system dynamics together.

In Chapter 3, it is trying exploratory research with the causal map of system dynamics for the existing studies on the exchange risk and exchange risk management. The companies' structures have been analyzed by the causal map of system dynamics. Through this, this study confirms that the results can be derived differently by the exchange rate depending on the structural problems that each company has.

The paper explains the exchange exposure determinants that have been described in the papers published in Korea, and a variety of cause-and-effect relationships that occurs in the exchange exposure mitigation strategies, considering with system dynamics. Through this, it tries to overcome the limitations in the existing exchange exposure studies and in the empirical analysis.

The exchange exposure mitigation strategy, after the foreign exchange crisis, has been recognized very important issue in the practice to the domestic companies, and companies are looking for a variety of methods. Korean companies are now as much recognized in the world, the study of exchange exposure of Korean companies is considered to be treated with weighted in international journals in the future.

In Chapter 4, by developing the study in Chapter 3, it attempts the simulation of derivatives. Through it, the simulations helps us to understand the structure of the company. And this chapter presents a model that can predict the benefits associated with the exchange rate fluctuation, and performs simulation work in the center of financial derivatives related to exchange rate.

Companies often trade the financial derivatives as hedge purposes of exchange risk (Kim & Ban 2004). Thus, as the domestic companies increase foreign trades, the exchange exposure has increased, and many companies have managed the exchange risk through derivatives. As a result, derivatives market has also grown rapidly. Due to the characteristic of the country with high foreign dependence, many domestic companies in Korea are receiving management effects by the exchange rate fluctuation (Kwon & Hwang 1999). For these exchange risk, most of companies are taking exchange hedge, and they are using derivatives as means of such exchange hedge.

It is because it can see how the effect of derivatives is showing actual impact on the companies before and after the financial crisis. Companies have also used as investing means, without using the derivatives as the original function of the exchange risk hedge. In such a case, the derivatives for exchange risk management have also become dangerous goods that extremely increase the exchange risk. This is because the companies use the derivatives with lacking in understanding.

This Chapter tries to research the structure of companies' derivatives by system dynamics, and discover the structural problems held by KIKO product, a kind of derivatives. And, it tries to check the risk of exchange rates fluctuations throughout the simulation. Through this, it can look at that how the wrong confidence of companies for the exchange rate fluctuation can critically affect the corporate finance.

In Chapter 5, it presents an empirical study. During the period of 2003 to 2010, at the times of Korea financial crisis, it analyzes the profits of the company by the exchange rate fluctuation through a panel analysis. This could confirm that the profits of the companies can be affected by the exchange rate fluctuation and foreign currency assets of the companies.

By using the 8-year data of 443 listed companies and registered companies, it can weigh up the influence of companies in overall. Also, it is compared by dividing into sub-period 1 (2003 to 2006) and sub-period 2 (2007 to 2010). Through this, it can look at whether the derivatives to be used for exchange risk management have played the key role in hedge.

In Chapter 6, it explains the meaning and limitation that the previous chapters own. Many contributions in the academic and practical fields are found in this book, together.

Through this study, companies can understand that the exchange rate fluctuation affects the various structures on the corporate finance, and through system dynamics technique, it is understood that it is possible to predict even the financial behavior of companies through simulation even from the companies. Moreover, through systematic thinking, it is possible for corporate investors to analyze structure that the company originally has, and can allow for simulation of the external shocks. I hope that studies like these can be developed to a new study field as well as in the financial field.

II Literature Review

1. The consideration of the previous studies

This book has handled the study on the corporate finance related to the exchange rate. The existing exchange exposure studies have been related to the exchange rate are made up of mainly empirical analysis and case studies. The empirical analysis and case studies described the single line relationship for the exchange exposure and determinants of exchange exposure, and they, in relation to exchange exposure mitigation strategy, presented a variety of strategies. However, there are some limitations of these studies. Since the impact by the exchange rate is different by the time, and different depending on the companies' structure, the dynamic analysis should be considered more effectively.

Recently, as well as linear research methods, many academic researches use nonlinear studies to analyze how various environmental factors have an impact. In particular, the system dynamics approach has been used in various fields. System dynamics has been used in the engineering sector, and it is used in the medical field. Also, it has been developed in the area of business dynamics. Here, by utilizing the system dynamics, I was trying to study for the strategy of foreign exchange risk. This book presents two theories. In this book, causal relationship can be understood through the study on the exchange exposure and exchange exposure mitigation strategies, and examines the studies on the impact of companies by the exchange rate fluctuation. Furthermore, it tries to examine the study on system dynamics methodology. System dynamics, for the subject with the dynamics, is a study that researches the causal loop relationship.

This study, for the effects of exchange rate fluctuation and corporate finance, shows that system dynamics study method is appropriate.

2. Theoretical background of Foreign Exchange Exposure and FX Risk Management Strategy

Since Adler & Dumas (1984a) showed how to measure foreign currency exposure through the skewness of exchange rate fluctuation variable in the linear regression equation, the full-fledged research on the foreign currency exposure started. They considered the sensitivity to the changes in the value caused by exchange rate fluctuation as the foreign currency exposure and enabled a detailed empirical analysis. Through his research concerning American companies, Jorion (1990) confirmed that the exchange rate fluctuation affected the enterprise value, depending on the proportion of export.

Khoo (1994) analyzed the foreign currency exposure that occurred in Australian companies due to payment for machinery and facility in foreign currency. Donnelly & Sheehy (1996) analyzed the foreign currency exposure of the British exporters. The research on foreign currency exposure developed into the alleviation strategy of foreign currency exposure for the companies to prevent the decrease in their value caused by foreign currency exposure.

Bodnar, Hayt, & Marston (1998) investigated and studied the foreign currency hedging of American companies against the exposure to foreign currency. Miller (1998) introduced the strategies of multi-national companies to hedge against the risks through overseas production. Miller and Reuer (1998) proved that the large companies alleviate the level of foreign currency exposure through foreign direct investment.

Many Korean companies had been quite insensitive to the changes in the enterprise value caused by the exchange rate fluctuation before the 1997 Asian financial crisis. It was because the government defended against the drastic change in the exchange rate. However, since the financial crisis, they have witnessed that the exchange rate fluctuation has serious effects not only on the companies, but also on the survival of the country. Therefore, since 1997, many papers on the foreign currency exposure have been published, and many researches have been carried out in Korea. The exchange rate, which used to be studied mainly from the economic perspective, has started to be researched in the field of business administration studies.

After the Asian financial crisis in 1997, papers have been conducted regarding the exposure, actively. Kwon (1998), while research on the effect of currencies and asymmetry in estimating foreign currency exposure, conducted a full-scale study. Kwon (1999a), with the KOSPI 200 companies, studied the scale effects and the characteristics of foreign exchange exposure characteristics, liquidity and currency risk exposure. In addition, Kwon (1999b) was trying to empirical analysis on the relationship between foreign exchange exposure and the cost of financial unstability. The foreign exchange risk increased hedge ratio, turnover margin, total asset turnover ratio, equity ratio, and the relationship with the unstability of financial status.

Ji & Kim (1999) explained foreign exchange rate and stock price. Lee (1999) studied the relationship between foreign exchange exposure and characteristic variables of the Korean firms and industries. And Park (2001) researched the exchange rate volatility and the Korean exports. Kim & Park (2003) studied the relationship between foreign exchange risk of multinational corporations and their ADR and underlying stock returns.

Kim (2003) researched effects on expected default risk of small-sized firms induced by drastic changes of foreign exchange rate during the Korea's financial crisis with non-financial firms listed on the Korea Stock Exchange from 1997 to 2000. Lee (2004) carried out an analysis of the foreign exchange exposure and determinants through non-financial firms listed on the Korea Stock Exchange from 1987 to 2001. Yi (2004a) estimated exchange exposure of Korea's firms on dollar, and Bian, Park, & Cho (2006) studied exchange rate exposure of Korean companies during around the period of economic crisis.

After financial crisis, Kang (2009) analyzed corporate cash flow exposures to foreign exchange rate and the determinants with companies listed on KRX and registered on KOSDAQ between 2000 and 2008. Nam & Xu (2011) reviewed The foreign currency risk and firm value with the non-financial firms listed on KRX from July 2005 to June 2009.

Lately, Park, & Chang (2013) reviewed the exchange rate and interest rate exposures of Korean corporations with non-financial 233 firms listed on KRX between 1990 and 2011. Cho, Bian, & Park (2013) analyzed currency crises and exchange rate exposure through 2116 firms of 23 countries around the currency crises in the 1990s.

Exposure mitigation strategies made many papers on thesis identified a causal relationship with the determinants of foreign exchange exposure. Also I could see about corporate strategy through the economics' papers. Exposure has not been explained just simply with the description of the independent variables and the dependent variables. Many companies consider a variety of strategies to prevent the decline in corporate value due to foreign exchange exposure. The mitigation strategies of foreign exchange exposure accordingly making a difference in the internal and external environment are diverse and make progress overall. The strategy can be divided into three areas as financial strategy operating strategy, pricing strategy (Bartram et al., 2010; Jeong, 2011).

Gwag, Chung, Sin, & Choe (2003) with respect to the exposure determinants, argued the need for the mitigation strategies along with analysis. Kwon & Joo (2004) has shown the need for a risk management system for companies, with the study on the characteristics and foreign exchange risk management practices from companies in Yeosu Industrial Complex.

The only research on the literature review of foreign currency exposure in Korea was carried out by Chung & Cho (2011). which was based on the papers published overseas. Chung & Cho (2011) divided the papers on foreign currency exposure into the factors that determined the level of foreign currency exposure and the others on the foreign currency management to alleviate the foreign currency exposure risks. However, they did not include the papers published in Korea, and therefore, there was no research that summed up the local papers. Therefore, this book summarizes the causal relationship based on the locally published papers, and aims to take a comprehensive look at the researches on the factors that determine the level of foreign currency exposure and the alleviation strategies of the foreign currency exposure of Korean companies.

There is various financial strategies for FX risk management. Many companies use the derivatives as the financial strategy, mainly. Roh, Yun, & Kim (1998) reviewed international hedging under concurrent risks of input and output prices and exchange rate with the case of Korean oil refinery. Yun (1998) studied exchange risk management with futures and option. Kim & Jeon (2001) analyzed economic measurement and management on foreign exchange exposure for manufacturing companies. Kwon (2006b) researched the exchange exposure and the maximum exchange loss in exchange risk analysis with non-financial firms listed on KRX between 1990 and 1997. Kwon, Chang, & Jung (2010) reviewed The usage of currency derivatives of the Korean firms and their management of the foreign exchange rate exposure. Recently, Kwon, & Park (2013) studied derivatives hedging, earnings management, and foreign exchange exposure. In addition, Kim, Kim, & Park (2013) analyzed hedging, liquidity constraints and investment through non-financial firms listed on Korea exchange between 2000 and 2009.

There are many studies about some operation strategies of foreign exchange risk. Chung (2001) studied foreign exchange exposure management of the Korean automobile companies. And Shin (2003) researched the impact of capital market imperfections and exchange rate uncertainty on corporate investment. Kwon (2009) analyzed internal transactions within business group and management of foreign exchange exposure. Kim (2011) studied the effect of the interaction between FDI location and product differentiation on the foreign exchange exposure. Jeong & Chung (2012) carried out the study of foreign exchange exposure of Korean firms and its relationship with foreign investors` investment.

Many companies use many pricing strategies for the management of foreign exchange risk. Kwon & Hwang (1999a) analyzed of characteristics of mark-up adjustment from FX fluctuation on export industry in Korea. Kim (2002b) studied The pricing-to-market effects of exchange rate with residual demand with monthly data of export over from January 1990 to March 2001. In addition, Kwak (2004) studied exchange rate pass-through and import prices in Korea`s manufacturing industries. Park & Cheong (2006) studied on countermeasure of export small and medium sized companies from FX fluctuation through survey of 407 export companies on 2005. Kwon & Joo (2011) studied the expected and observed exchange rate exposure of Korean firms. Recently, Choi & Ham (2013) analyzed the pass-through on Korean export prices of exchange rate changes with export price of Korea, price of competing country, FX rate on competing country, producer price index of Korea, exchange rate of Won, USA business barometer, the data from the bank of Korea between 2008 and 2011.

The papers of foreign exchange exposure have been reviewed. Many papers come from the study of liner causal relationship. It could be the limitation of the existing researches. But this book aims to develop the research on foreign currency exposure to another dimension through taking a comprehensive look at the circular causal relations that have not been discovered by the previous individual studies.

3. Theoretical background of System Dynamics

System dynamics has a grasp of the social system as multi-loop nonlinear feedback system (Forrester, 1993). In particular, it forecasts an unexpected change in a proactive process by modeling with the observed. And it helps making decisions and contributes to overcome the error of determination from liner thinking method.

System Dynamics was started by Jay Forrester, a professor at MIT in the 1960s and developed into Industrial dynamics, Urban dynamics, Business dynamics (Chung & Lee, 2012). Luhmann (1995) and Bertalanffy (1967) presented General System Theory. Waldrop (1992) and Kauffamn (1993) made effects to the Science of Complexity of development (Kim et al., 1999).

Bertalanffy (1976) pointed out that the system was made up of the components with dynamic interaction, and helped to find out the rules to control the pattern of the parts and process of the system. These made effects to cybernetics, systems dynamics, complexity science.

Donella, Dennis, Jørgen, & William (1972) claimed that the growth was not good always through 'The Limits to Growth: A Report For the Club of Rome's Project on the Predicament of Mankind. Because the exponential growth of the industry and the population will have a significant burden on the earth's capacity, which was concerned that it will be the predicament of mankind.

David Lane (1996) studied in the feedback structure. System Dynamics is to find the root cause of the dynamic changes in the feedback structure. The causal relationship between the feedback variables are interconnected structure means that form a closed circuit. (Richardson, 1991).

Peter Senge (1990) explained the system with only causal loop map and the crucial roles in systems thinking by applying it to business management. In his book, He made the book of the fifth discipline which described in the art and practice of learning organization. This book has become an important book for learning organization.

In Korea, researches on the system dynamics were released mainly through the Korea System Dynamics Review. Kim (2000) introduced systems thinking and causal maps of the first issue of the Korea System Dynamics Review. Moon & Seo (2000) showed patterns of future situations and problems using a system dynamics simulation (Hong & Jung, 2007).

Kim & Hong (2005) described the regulatory policy of the government with the view of systems thinking. It was explained that the problem can be so obsessed in the government's regulatory policy with phenomenon rather than a fundamental problem, which continues to create problems. And Jeong & Kim (2009) suggested the problems and solutions of causal maps through the study of limits and improvements from the analysis and design of causal loops. Through this study, a causal map was developed into a reliable research on various studies.

For systematic thinking, holistic thinking, feedback and time-based thinking are required (Kim, 2008). It has its characteristics to form a causal relationship between each component and analyze dynamic structures to understand the whole system, detect problems and find out solutions (Kim, Moon, & Kim, 1999; Jung & Kim, 2009). This systems thinking includes the contents related to cybernetics, information theory, game theory, and network theory.

About system dynamics, three things must be considered in order to create a causal loop diagram (Jung & Kim, 2009). First, all of the causal variables (independent variables) and result variables (dependent variables) should be changed. Second, after a variable that is a cause changes firstly, all the values of result variables (dependent variables) should be changed. Third, causal relationship should be verified while excluding other variables (third exogenous variable) not belong to causal variables or result variables (Chung & Lee, 2012).

If a causal relationship is established through the three processes, it needs to clearly determine whether it is in a positive or negative relationship. This means that we need to understand each circular structure is R loop or B loop and through this, solutions to address problems can be found in the connection between R loop and B loop. While quantitative research has a limitation to show single ladder aspect, system dynamics regard the whole as a feedback structure in which each variable affects each other in a dual ladder aspect. The more the companies are engaged in sales, the more they are exposed to foreign exchange. That is why they hedge foreign exchange to maintain the value of a company.

Dynamic analysis seems more appropriate to analyze such activities, rather than static analysis. Kwon. (2013) argued that the reason there were not so many studies that adopted system dynamics in the financial market is that traditional economists and financial specialists were not comfortable with the system dynamics originated from engineering.

III Exploratory Study: Systems Thinking Approach

1. Purpose and need of the research

Korean companies are actively carrying out their business in the global market and are using various currencies, including Korean won, as a means for payment. In case which a Korean company uses a currency other than KRW in transaction, it is subject to the risk related to accounting loss or decrease in company value caused by exchange rate fluctuation. Sometimes, the loss caused by the fluctuation affects the survival of a company. The bankruptcy of many Korean companies during the Asian financial crisis in 1997 was both directly and indirectly affected by the drastic fluctuation of the exchange rate (Kim, 2003). Even before the financial crisis, the research on the impact of the exchange rate on the national economy existed in the field of economics. However, after the 1997 financial crisis, the scope of the research expanded into the impact of the exchange rate fluctuation to corporate management. Since then, focused on foreign currency exposure, many researches have been carried out. The alleviation strategy of foreign currency exposure is to decrease the company's foreign currency exposure through managing the risk deriving from the exposure. Some papers have transformed the alleviation strategy of foreign currency exposure into the management strategy of foreign currency risk.

It is difficult to explain the change in the company value caused by foreign currency exposure in a simple manner. Many researches have estimated the foreign currency exposure based on PER (Price Earnings Ratio) affected by foreign currency fluctuation (Kwon, 1999a). However, they could not analyze the positive and negative effect from the various factors that determined foreign currency exposure. There were many cases where it was difficult to get a meaningful result because the determinant factors were offset against each other (Song & Cho, 2011). Therefore, simple empirical research has limitation in explaining such effect. Various offset effects from the exchange rate fluctuation may be estimated based on the company's structure, including the level of globalization, business size, foreign currency liability ratio, dividend payment rate, and level of liquidity (Yu & Hong, 2009). Even though the size of the foreign currency exposure is small, the exposure may be increased by dramatic fluctuation in the exchange rate. In addition, the size of the impact from the increase and decrease in the exchange rate to the company may have a great diversity because of the asymmetry of the foreign currency exposure (Lee, 2003).

this book will explain the various causal relations between the factors that determine the foreign currency exposure and the alleviation strategies of foreign currency exposure explained by the papers registered by the Korean Citation Index based on the system dynamics mind-set. This book will try to overcome the limitation in the foreign currency exposure researches that are difficult to be explained through only empirical analysis. The alleviation strategy of foreign currency exposure are not only valued in the academic field, but also in the business, and the companies are looking for various ways to alleviate the foreign currency exposure.

Therefore, this research will draw a comprehensive causal loop diagram that shows the structural causal relations between the factors discovered from the previous studies that determine foreign currency exposure and the strategy to alleviate the exposure. It is believed that this will help systematically understand the causal relationship between the foreign currency exposure and the strategy to alleviate the exposure. Since the analyzed papers were mostly dealing with the manufacturing businesses, the scope of this study will also be limited to the manufacturing business.

2. Study methodology

2.1 Direction of study

There were many papers related to exchange rate. But this research focused on corporate's financial effects about the papers registered by the Korean Citation Index. In addition, since the research on the foreign currency exposure started in a full-fledged way after the Asian financial crisis in 1997, only the papers published after 1998 were studied. Under this standard, 72 papers from 23 academic journals were selected to be studied, as explained in <Table 1>. If you take a look at <Table 1>, you may see that the largest number of papers (15) is from the International Business Journal. 10 papers were from the Korean Journal of Financial Management, and 7 from the Journal of International Trade and Industry Studies. That may be because the foreign currency exposure is a meaningful subject in international business management, financial management, and global trade. And we can assume that the foreign currency exposure are related to many fields trough various journals which were published with it. The largest number of papers were published right after the 1997 Asian financial crisis, and the number is on the increase after the global financial crisis in 2008, and it seems that the changes in the external environment caused by the exchange rate has affected the researchers as well. The studies relevant to foreign currency exposure are also vibrantly carried out after 2011.

This study divides the relevant papers into the ones on the factors that determine the foreign currency exposure and the others on the alleviation strategy of foreign currency exposure. Such division was applied to the study of Bartram, Brown, & Minton (2010) and Chung & Cho (2011) and is a general trend in the research on foreign currency exposure.

<Table 1> Papers on foreign currency exposure (after 1998, by published year and academic journal)

Year	1998	1999	2000	2001	2002	2003	2004	2006	2007	2008	2009	2010	2011	2012	2013	Total
International Business Journal		2	1	1	1	1	1	1	2		2		2		1	15
The Koean Journal of Financial Management		3				1	1			1	1	2		1		10
Journal of International Trade and Industry Studies				1		2	2			1			1			7
Korea Trade Review	2	1				1		1								5
Korean Journal of Futures and Options	1												1		2	5
Korean management review		1		1	1			1						1		5
Journal of Industrial Economics and Business				1				1			2					4
Journal of Economics Studies							1								1	2
Korean Journal of Financial Studies													1		1	2
Journal of Korean Economic Analysis				1									1			2
Journal of Money & Finance				1		1										2
International Tusiness Review												1			1	2
Kukje Kyungje Yongu					1		1									2
Korean Journal of Financial Engineering								1								1
Journal of the Aviation Management Society of Korea															1	1
The Korean-Japanese Jounal of Economics and Management Studies													1			1
Korean Accounting Review														1		1
Journal of Shipping and Logistics							1									1
International Commerce and Information Review													1			1
Korean Journal of Accounting Information													1			1
International Area Studies Review														1		1
The Korean Journal of Economic Studies					1											1
Korean Journal of Small Tusiness Studies						1										1
Total	3	7	1	6	4	7	7	5	2	2	5	3	9	4	7	72

2.2 Dilemma of study on exchange rate

In accordance with the papers published overseas that applied the previous foreign currency exposure research method, the impact from the foreign currency exposure was significant in 10 to 25% of the companies in each country. (Bodnar & Wong, 2003) Most companies set the adequate strategy to alleviate the foreign currency exposure and respond, once the size of the exposure increases. Therefore, it is difficult to ignore the possibility where the affect from the foreign currency exposure itself will not seem significant because the companies decrease the impact from the exposure through the alleviation strategy of foreign currency exposure. In addition, since there are elements that have positive and negative impact, depending on the factor to determine the foreign currency exposure, it may be difficult to have a meaningful result, since the impact from the elements are offset against each other. Moreover, in case the company manages the foreign currency risk in a proper manner, the foreign currency exposure may seem statistically meaningless. Depending on its own business activities, each company has different factors to determine the foreign currency exposure and according to such factors, it would have a strategy to alleviate the foreign currency exposure. In case the companies perfectly hedge against the fluctuation in the exchange rate, the foreign currency exposure will be zero. In case the hedging is incomplete, depending on the direction of foreign currency fluctuation, the value of the foreign currency exposure may be either negative (-) or positive (+). That is because in case an exporter carries out complete hedging through derivatives, the exposure may temporarily seem meaningless, if it is assessed based on the previous foreign currency exposure measurement method. Therefore, since the impact from the foreign currency exposure is created based on complex causal relations, the research should be carried out to take a comprehensive approach and look at the causal relationship between the elements, instead of trying to understand the relationship in a simple manner.

2.3 Study model

The most representative indicator to understand the corporate activities is the financial statement. This research aimed to build the basic model for the causal relationship model through the income statement, which is one of the financial statements. In accordance with the Generally Accepted Accounting Principle 2.44 of Korea Accounting Standard Board (based on November 27, 2009 resolution), "Income statement is a financial report that provides the information on the company's business performance for a certain time period. Income statement not only represents the business performance of the applicable accounting period, but also provides the information useful to forecast the company's future cash flow, ability to generate profit, etc." Through this definition, it may be assumed that the income statement represents the circular, causal structure of the corporate activities because the corporate activities may be forecast based on the income statement. Companies carry out activities to generate sales. Sales are generated through this corporate activity. Subsequently, cost of sales, operating expenses, non-operating profit, and corporate tax expenses occur. Lastly, net income occurs. Once again, the net income is invested in the operating activities to generate sales.

Previous researches mainly used PER (Price Earnings Ratio) for the research of the foreign currency exposure. However, as it was represented in <Figure 2>, this research used the net income for dynamic analysis. Since the net income of the company is directly related to PER (Paek, Lee, & Park, 2001), there will be no major problem even though it is used as a replacement for PER to indicate the corporate value. In accordance with the Generally Accepted Accounting Principle of Korea Standard Accounting Board, the net income in the income statement is the value calculated through subtracting cost of sales, operating expenses, non-operating profit, and income tax expenses from sales. Net income boosts the sales activities, and the sales increase again. From a circular and causal standpoint, the "R LOOP", which is a cycle consists of sales → gross margin(+) → operating profit(+) → income before tax(+) → net income(+) → sales activities(+) → sales quantity(+) → sales(+), is created. It may be understood that the management's business activities to secure net income through generating sales are creating the R Loop. R Loop is the reinforcement loop of growth. Companies try to continue to grow up. They increase their sales and sizes through the growth loop. But there are limitation on the growth. Other loops limit the growth loop. The cost of sales increases with the increase in the production cost, and it creates the B1 Loop that decreases (-) the net income. The production cost is caused by the complex manufacturing mechanism, and here, the purchase cost, production labor cost, and R&D cost were considered as variables. It was shown that even though R&D cost increased the operating expenses, it increased the productivity, and ultimately, decreased the production cost. In addition, in the B2 Loop, vigorous sales activities increase the operating expenses and decrease the operating profit. Also, there is B3 Loop, where the net income decreases (-) due to the increase in the corporate tax expenses. This research referred to the causal relationship built by Sterman (2000) that the causal relationship relevant to the sales quantity was affected by price comparison and market demand, depending on the selling price. Selling price is also dependent on the company's price strategy; however, ultimately, it is affected by the production cost. Overall, it turns the loop R, and affect to rotate small loops in each area. The revenue makes the loop related to the selling price. Costs of sales include the loop that affect costs associated with sales. Operating expense makes its loop related to operating income. These small loops make effects to other loops with the company's R Loop, which will receive the impact from all loops.

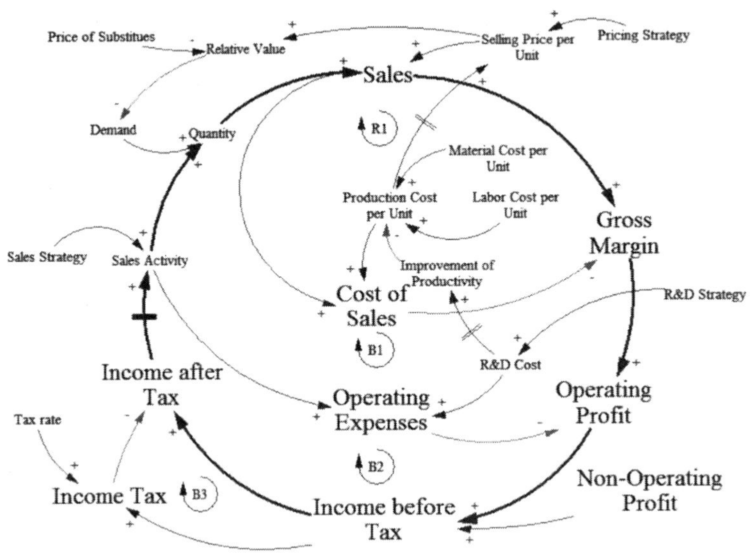

<Figure 2> Casual loop diagram on corporate activities based on income statement

Based on this, the causal loop diagram on the corporate activities may be drawn, as was represented in <Figure 2>. <Figure 2> assumes that the sales activities will become more active, once the net income increases. Intuitively speaking, in case the net income increases, the management will increase the sales activities further to generate even more net income. However, in case the sales activities are increasing, the operating expenses will increase. Once the marketing activities are strengthened to increase the sales quantity, the marketing cost must increase. In addition, if selling price increases, the sales will immediately increase. However, the sales quantity may decrease through customers' act to compare prices. This shows the mechanism of the "invisible hands" of Adam Smith.

3. Building of Causal Loop Diagram on exchange rate exposure

3.1 The causal loop diagram on the determinants of exchange rate exposure

In 1998, after the 1997 Asian financial crisis, many small and mdium sized enterprises in Korea were faced with the threat of bankruptcy because their corporate value was affected by the exchange rate. In addition, since much attention was given to the exchange rate after the Asian financial crisis, the studies on the foreign currency exposure started in a full-fledged way in the academic field.

In this chapter, the papers that were focused on the factors that determined the foreign currency exposure will be reviewed. If you take a look at <Table 2>, you may find the papers that were mainly focused on the foreign currency exposure. Kwon (1999b) stated that the foreign currency exposure have direct impact on the corporate value through the empirical analysis on the relationship between the foreign currency exposure and financial distress cost. Lee (1999) analyzed the relationship between the foreign currency exposure of the Korean companies and industries and the attribute variable. Lee (2004) studied the foreign currency exposure of different currencies through the estimation of Korean companies' exposure to USD and JPY. Nam & Xu (2011) studied the foreign currency risk and company value. <Table 2> introduces main causal relationships explained by each paper. In the case of exporters, negative (-) relationship to decrease the foreign currency exposure is created by revenue and foreign currency liability ratio.

<Table 2> Causal relationship in foreign currency exposure

Reference	Cause and Effect Relationship	Subject of Research	Object of Research
Kwon, T. (1998)	Foreign Exchange Exposure -> Company Value(-)	The Effect of Currencies and Asymmetry in Estimating Foreign Currency Exposure	KOSPI 559 Companies between 1990~1996
Kwon, T. (1999a)	FX Fluctuation -> Company Value(-) Lagged Effect, Size, Flutuation -> Foreign Exchange Exposure(+)	The Charcteristics of the Foreign Currency Exposure of the KOSPI 200 Firms and Non-KOSPI 200 Firms	460 of Korean Manufacturing Companies between 1990 and 1996
Kwon, T. (1999b)	Foreign Currency Exposure -> Hedge(+), Growth Rate, Assets Turnover Rate, Equity Rate -> Corporate Distress(-), Foreign Exchange Exposure -> Financial Weakness(-)	An Empirical Study on the Relationship between Foreign Exchange Exposure and Cost of Financial Distress	Korean Manufacturing Companies between 1992 and 1998
Kwon, T., & Park, J. (1999)	Import Ratio -> Foreign Exchange Premium(+)	Relationship between Foreign Exchange Risk Premiums and Firm Characteristics in the Korean Stock Market	460 of Korean Manufacturing Companies between 1990 and 1996
Kwon, T., & Hwang, H. (1999b)	Size -> Foreign Exchange Exposure(+)	The Characteristics of Currency Exposure in Korean Manufacturing Companies	460 of Korean Manufacturing Companies between 1990 and 1996
Ji, H., & Kim, Y. (1999)	Foreign Exchange Exposure -> Stock Price(+)	Causal Relation between Stock Markets and Foreign Exchange Market : The International Evidence	FX rate and Stock price between 1980 and 1997
Lee, H. (1999)	Corporate Size and Cash Capability -> Foreign Exchange Exposure(+)	The Relationship between Foreign Exchange Exposure and Characteristic Variables of the Korean Firms and Industries	291 Companies listed on KRX between 1987 and 1997
Park, S. (2001)	FX Fluctuation -> Export(+)	Exchange Rate Volatoility and the Korean Exports	Monthly Exchange Rate and Export data and Economic index from Bank Of Korea
Kim, D., & Park, S. (2003)	Foreign Exchange Exposure-> Company Value by Industry(-)	The Relationship between Foreign Exchage Risk of Multinational Coreportations and Their ADR and Underlysing Stock Returns	8 Firms on Advanced Country between 1993 and 1998 and 5 Firms on Developing Country between 1994 and 1998
Kim, Y. (2003)	Foreign Exchange Exposure -> Bankrupcy Possibility(+)	Effects on Expected Default Risk of Small-sized Firms Induced by Drastic Changes of Foreign Exchange Rate during the Korea's Financial Crisis	Non-financial firms listed on the Korea Stock Exchange from 1997 to 2000
Lee, H. (2003)	Foreign Exchange Exposure -> Rate of Return(+) : Asymmetrics on Foreign Exchange Exposure	The Foreign Exchange Exposure and Asymmetrics on Individual Firms	260 of Non-financial firms listed on the Korea Stock Exchange from 1987 to 2007
Lee, H. (2004)	Company Size -> Foreign Exchange Exposure(-), Export비중 -> Asymmetricss on Foreign Exchange Exposure(+), Long Term Liability -> Exchange Risk Management(+) -> Foreign Exchange Exposure(-)	An Analysis of The Foreign Exchange Exposure and Determinants	Non-financial firms listed on the Korea Stock Exchange from 1987 to 2001

Yi, C. (2004a)	Foreign Exchange Exposure -> Rate of Return(+)	Estimation of Exchange Exposure of Korea's Firms on Dollar and Yen	23 Firms of Auto and Electronics Industry between 1992 and 2002
Kwon, T. (2006a)	Export Ratio -> Foreign Exchange Exposure(+), Foreign Currency Liability Rate -> Foreign Exchange Exposure(-) Direct Investment Rate on Overseas -> Foreign Exchange Exposure(-)	Lagged Exchange Rate Exposure and Determinants of Exchange Rate Exposure	388 of Manufacturing Companies listed on KRX between 1998 and 2003
Bian, A., Park, K., & Cho, J. (2006)	Company Size -> Foreign Exchange Exposure(-), Company Size(Size), Growth Rate(BM), Dividend Rate(DIV) -> Foreign Exchange Exposure(-), Quick Ratio(QR) -> Foreign Exchange Exposure(+)	Exchange Rate Exposure of Korean Companies: Pre- and Post- Economic Crisis Analysis	Manufacturing Companies listed on KRX between 1994 and 2002
Kwon, T. (2007)	Foreign Currency Liability Rate -> Asymmetric Foreign Exchange Exposure(+), Export -> Asymmetric Foreign Exchange Exposure(-), Foreign Currency Liability Rate, Export -> Natural Hedge	Asymmetric Exchange Rate Exposure and Foreign Currency Denominated Debt	Non-Financial Companies listed on KRX between 1990 and 2004
Park, J., Kwon, T., & Lee, W. (2008)	Foreign Investors -> Selling/Purchasing Trade(+)	Foreign Investors Response to the Foreign Exchange Rate Risk in the Korean Stock Markets	Tradin Volume and Ordering Volume on Stock Market
Kang, W. (2009)	Company Size -> Foreign Exchange Exposure(-), Company Size -> Foreign Exchange Exposure Hedge Strategy, Finacial Hardness -> Foreign Exchange Exposure(+), Cash Flow -> Foreign Exchange Exposure(+)	Corporate Cash Flow Exposures to Foreign Exchange Rate and the Determinants : Korean Listed Non-financial Firms	Companies listed on KRX and registered on KOSDAQ between 2000 and 2008
Yu, S. & Hong, H. (2009)	Internationalized Ratio, Company Size, Dividend Rate -> Foreign Exchange Exposure(+) Growth Possibility, Liability Ratio -> Hedging(+)	Foreign Exchange Exposure of Korean Firms	500 Non-financial firms listed on the Korea Stock Exchange from 1999 to 2001 and 536 firms from 2002 to 2005
Lee, H., & Park, S. (2009)	Export Firms-> Foreign Exchange Exposure(+)	Foreign Exchange Exposure and Its Determinants of Korean Listed Companies	Non-Financial Companies listed on KRX between 1999 and 2007
Nam, G., & Xu, H. (2011)	FX Risk -> Company Value(-)	The Foreign Currency Risk and Firm Value	The non-financial firms listed on KRX from July 2005 to June 2009
Lee, S., & Choi, Y. (2011)	Foreign Exchange Exposure -> Export Volume(+), Export Price Change(+), Exchange Risk -> Company Value(-)	The Effects of Foreign Exchange Volatility on Export and Firm's Profit	1,080 firms listed on KRX and registered on KOSDAQ between 2000 and 2010
Huh, Y., & Park, S. (2011)	FX Fluctuation -> Foreign Exchange Exposure on Financial Statements(+), Foreign Exchange Exposure on Economy(+)	The Effect of Foreign Exchange Rate Changes on Firm Performance Forecast	Non-Financial 6,055 firms listed on KRX between 1992 and 2007
Park, J., & Change, B. (2013)	Export Ratio -> Foreign Exchange Exposure(+), Foreign Exchange Exposure -> International Movement of Capital(+)	The Exchange Rate and Interest Rate Exposures of Korean Corporations	Non-Financial 233 firms listed on KRX between 1990 and 2011
Cho, J., Bian, A., & Park, K. (2013)	FX Fluctuation -> Company Value(-)	Currency Crises and Exchange Rate Exposure	2116 firms 23 countires around the currency crises in the 1990s

Various factors in foreign currency exposure affect the enterprise value, and therefore, since the multiple factors with positive and negative effects are offset against each other, the impact from foreign currency exposure on enterprise value does not seem significant in many cases. Based on the impact from the exchange rate fluctuation on the share of bankrupt SMEs (Small and Medium Enterprises) during the Asian financial crisis, Kim (2003) explained that the foreign currency exposure might have fatal impact on the company, depending on the situation. Lee (2003) explained that due to asymmetry in foreign currency exposure, the extent of enterprise value caused by exchange rate fluctuation may vary. In addition, papers arguing that the factors that determined the foreign currency exposure in each company have serious impact on the company value have been published. Recently, Park & Chang (2013) studied the foreign currency and interest rate exposure of the public non-financial companies in Korea.

Based on the papers of the foreign currency exposure in <Table 2>, as shown in <Table 3>, a few types of foreign currency exposure may be discovered for each corporate type. This book has divided the impact into typical types through separating the sales and purchase, which are the basic corporate activities, taking place at home or abroad. However, there are following premises. In the case of overseas sales, since in most cases sales are made in foreign currency, foreign currency receivable occurs, and the proceeds from sales are paid in foreign currency. In the case where the company makes overseas purchase, since it makes purchase in foreign currency, foreign currency dominated liability occurs, and the company pays in foreign currency. In addition, it was assumed that the payment for the local sales and purchase were made in local currency and not in foreign currency. There are cases where overseas sales and purchase are made in KRW, or the local ones in foreign currency. However, such cases will not be dealt with in this book.

Because such cases are not common and may overly complicate the causal relationship. The foreign currency exposure in each of the four types has its distinctive features. Some conglomerate would qualify for more than a few types in <Table 3>. In their case, they may sell both at home and abroad and purchase both in Korea and in other countries. However, since such cases are caused by the combination of different types, they will not be dealt in this research because the purpose of this research is to simplify the types of complex foreign currency exposure to understand them in an easy manner. In the causal loop diagram, in the case of overseas sales, the selling price is shown in foreign currency, while in the case of local sales, the price is shown in KRW. In addition, in the case of overseas purchase, the purchase price is shown in foreign currency, while in the case of local purchase, the price is shown in KRW. This is to help the readers easily separate the currencies used in sales and purchase on the causal loop diagram.

<Table 3> Separation of foreign currency exposure impact, depending on corporate type

Overseas Sales	A Type	B Type
Domestic Sales	C Type	D Type
	Domestic Purchase	Overseas Purchase

The causal loop diagram of each type is shown in <Figure 3>, <Figure 4>, <Figure 5>, and <Figure 6>. Regarding the exchange rate, a variable, KRW to foreign currency exchange rate was used for better understanding of the causal loop diagram. This indicates that in case the USD to KRW exchange rate increases from KRW 1,000 per dollar to 1,100, the KRW to foreign currency exchange rate on the Casual loop diagram will increase (+). On the contrary, in case the rate decreases to KRW 900, the exchange rate on the map will decrease (-).

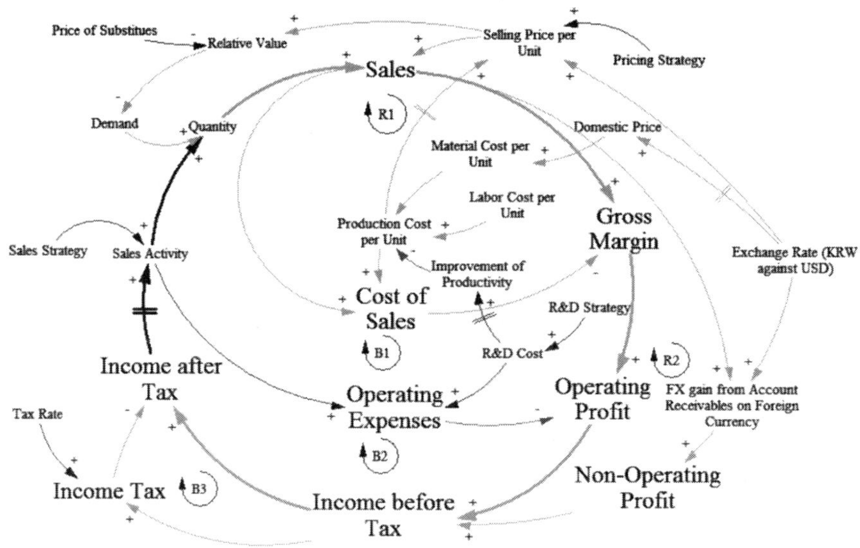

<Figure 3> Overseas sales, local purchase

In <Figure 3>, in case sales occur overseas, the exchange rate directly impacts the selling price in foreign currency (+). In case the USD to KRW exchange rate is KRW 1,000 per dollar, for the product that is sold at 1 dollar, the selling price in foreign currency represented on the income statement will be KRW 1,000. However, in case the rate is KRW 1,100 per dollar, the selling price in foreign currency represented on the income statement will be KRW 1,100. The selling price in foreign currency affects the sales (+), gross margin (+), and operating profit (+). As time goes by, the changes in the exchange rate affect the local price (+) and local purchase price (+).Since it takes time for the change in the exchange rate to affect the local price, its effect on sales is bigger and appears faster than its effect on operating profit (-) caused by the increase in purchase price. Meanwhile, unless the proceeds from sales are received in sales, sales receivable in foreign currency (+) will occur in the case of overseas sales. In the case of sales receivable in foreign currency, if the exchange rate increases at the time of actual payment after sales, foreign exchange gain (+) occur.

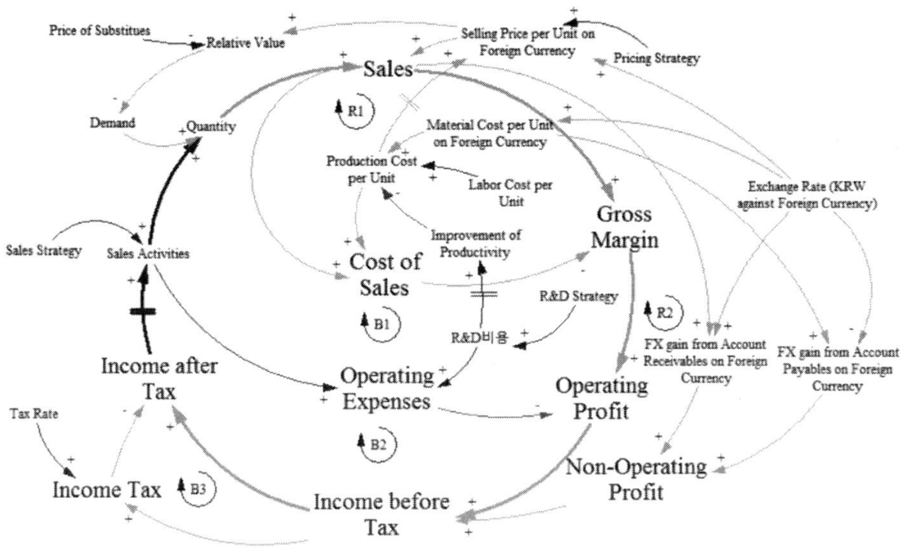

<Figure 4> Overseas sales and purchase

<Figure 4> indicates the case where both the sales and purchase occur overseas. The exchange rate fluctuation directly affects the sales and purchase price in foreign currency (+). As a result, exchange rate fluctuation affects the selling price in foreign currency (+) and gross margin (+). Meanwhile, exchange rate affects the purchase price in foreign currency (+), cost of sales (+), and gross margin (-). Receivable in foreign currency may occur due to overseas sales. In addition, payable in foreign currency may occur due to overseas purchase. In the case of payable in foreign currency, in case the exchange rate increases at the time of payment after purchase, foreign exchange loss occurs. Since both the sales and purchase are made in foreign currency, you may misunderstand that there is no foreign currency exposure. However, as shown in <Figure 4>, the foreign currency exposure affects the causal loop diagram in various ways.

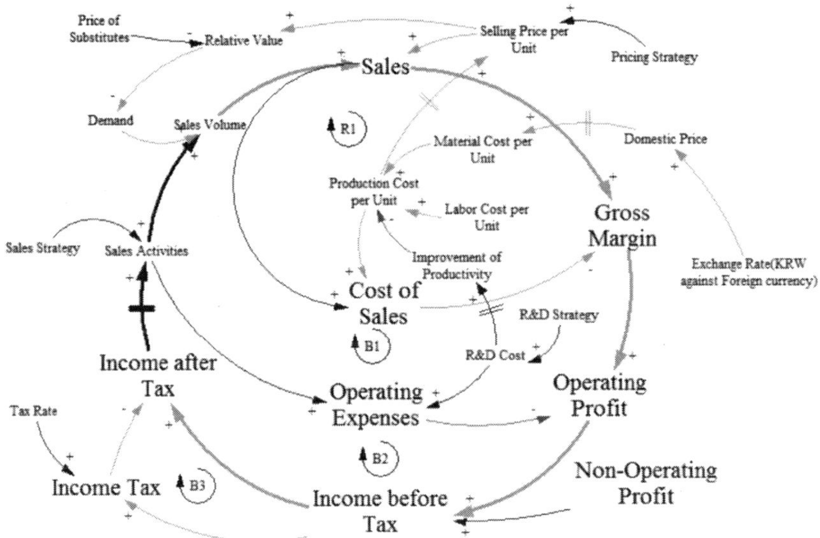

<Figure 5> Local sales and purchase

<Figure 5> indicates the case where the sales and purchase occur locally, there is no direct impact from exchange rate. However, after time delays, exchange rate affects the local price (+), and as a result, the purchase price in KRW changes. If it changes (+), the selling price (+) is affected over the long-term.

<Figure 6> indicates the case where the sales occur locally, and the purchase is made overseas. The changes in exchange rate directly affects the purchase price in foreign currency (+); due to the changes in the purchase price in foreign currency, cost of sales (+) is affected; as a result, it directly affects the operating profit (-). Therefore, in case the purchase price (+) changes, the production cost (+) and selling price (+) are affected. In addition, in the case of payable in foreign currency, in case the exchange rate increases at the time of payment after purchase, foreign exchange loss occurs. Through the causal loop diagram on foreign currency exposure above, you may see that the exchange rate fluctuation

affects not only the sales and purchase price, but also non-operating profit. In addition, even though there is no direct effect, the factors have no other option but to be affected by the exchange rate fluctuation after certain period of time. Additionally, depending on the type of the company, exchange rate fluctuation has either positive or negative impact on foreign currency exposure.

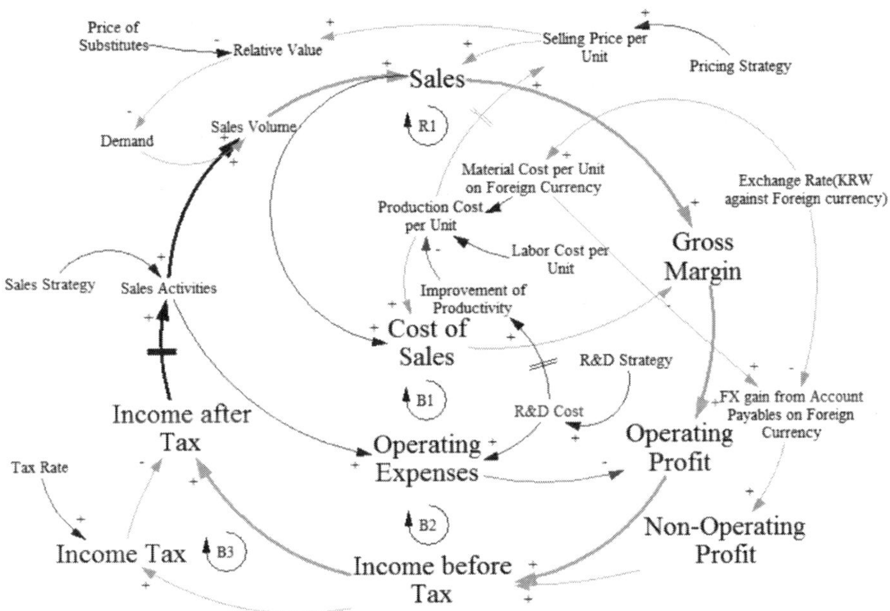

<Figure 6> Local sales and overseas purchase

3.2 The causal loop diagram on the determinants of hedging strategy on exchange rate exposure

As it was the case with the papers on the factors that determined the foreign currency exposure, there were many papers on the strategy to alleviate the foreign currency exposure that discovered the causal relationship. In addition, the corporate strategies could be understood through economics papers. Foreign currency exposure cannot be simply understood through the explanation on the independent and dependent variables because companies consider various strategies to prevent the decrease in the enterprise value caused by foreign currency exposure. The change in the foreign currency exposure caused by the change in the exchange rate provokes changes in the company's internal and external environment. As a result, the company carries out multiple comprehensive strategies to alleviate the foreign currency exposure. In their research on the peculiarities of the foreign currency risk of the companies in Yeosu Industrial Complex and the ways to manage such risk, Kwon & Joo (2004) showed the needs for the companies to implement the system to manage the foreign currency risk. Gwag, Chung, Sin, & Choe (2003) analyzed the factors that determined the foreign currency exposure and insisted that there was a need to implement the strategy to alleviate the foreign currency exposure. The strategy to defend the foreign currency exposure may be separated into financial strategy, operational strategy, and pricing strategy (Bartram et al., 2010; Chung & Cho, 2011).

<Table 4> summarized the number of papers on the foreign currency exposure strategy based on their subject. There were 29 papers on financial strategy, 9 on operational strategy, and 9 on pricing strategy. There were many researches on the financial strategy focused on derivatives, while the subject of the researches on operational strategy varied, including foreign investment (e.g., establishment of overseas factories) and foreign currency liabilities. The pricing strategy is a strategy to preserve the net income through increasing the selling price to respond to the cost increase factors caused by the change in exchange rate and offsetting such increase against cost pressure. In economics, there have been many researches on pricing. However, this book was focused on the nine papers that could directly explain the pricing strategy of companies. There were

papers that considered multiple strategies at the same time. However, this book considered the subject of the paper as financial strategy, in case the proportion of the financial strategy in the paper was relatively higher because such classification helped us understand each strategy. The causal loop diagram on each strategy was drawn based on type A, which indicated overseas sales and local purchase cases. That is because type A is the one most commonly found among local exporters and is effective to explain each strategy.

<Table 4> Classification of papers on the alleviation strategy of foreign currency exposure

Category	1998	1999	2000	2001	2002	2003	2004	2006	2007	2008	2009	2010	2011	2012	2013	Total
Financial Strategy	2		1	3	1	2	3	2	1		1	3	3	2	5	29
Operational Strategy				1	1	2				1	1		1	2		9
Pricing Strategy		1		1	2		2	1					2			9
Total	2	1	1	5	4	4	5	3	1	1	2	3	6	4	5	47

3.2.1 The causal loop diagram on financial strategy

Through the research on the foreign currency exposure of the companies that exported and invested overseas and the factors that affect their decision to hedge against the exposure, Yi (2001) discovered that the companies have financial strategies against the foreign currency exposure. In its research on the effective foreign currency risk management technique using derivatives products, Yun (2003) explained that the financial strategy utilizing derivatives was effective in alleviating the foreign currency exposure. Through the research on the exposure of the companies that had international transactions to foreign currency risk and the factors that affected the decision on the derivatives products to hedge the risk, Yi (2003) confirmed that the foreign currency risk decreased through derivatives. Recently, Kim, Kim, & Park (2013) studied the use of derivatives products by the companies through analyzing the investment cash flow sensitivity affected by the company's hedging activities.

<Figure 7> was prepared based on the relevant papers. When exchange rate increases, selling price increases. In addition, sales and operating profit will increase. Once time passes by after exchange rate increases, local price increases, and purchase price increases to decrease operating profit. When exchange rate decreases, sales price and sales drop to decrease gross margin. Since forward products are to hedge the exchange rate risk, it moves in the direction opposite to the change in sales price. When the company's operating profit decreases due to drop in exchange rate, the value of forward products increases to increase the non-operating profit. The reason that most of the papers on the financial strategy dealt with derivatives product could be explained through the fact that companies frequently used derivatives as part of their financial strategy. Structural understanding is required when the financial strategy is established in the companies. It is risky to develop the financial strategy using forward products without having understanding of foreign currency exposure. <Figure 7> indicates that even though there is time gap, the foreign currency exposure causes increase in the purchase price through the local price. In case only the sales price in foreign currency is considered over the short-term, forward products may alleviate the foreign currency exposure. However, it decreases gross margin over the long-term and such impact remains as the risk for the company. That is why the system dynamics thinking is required for foreign currency exposure and the strategy to alleviate the exposure. When considering various impacts from the foreign currency exposure through the causal loop diagram, financial strategy is simple, and the impact is limited. Unless the companies take an approach based on the systematic thinking, they will end up with a simple finan-

cial strategy. It may be understood that many researches reflected the reality of the actual business that focused mainly on the financial strategy.

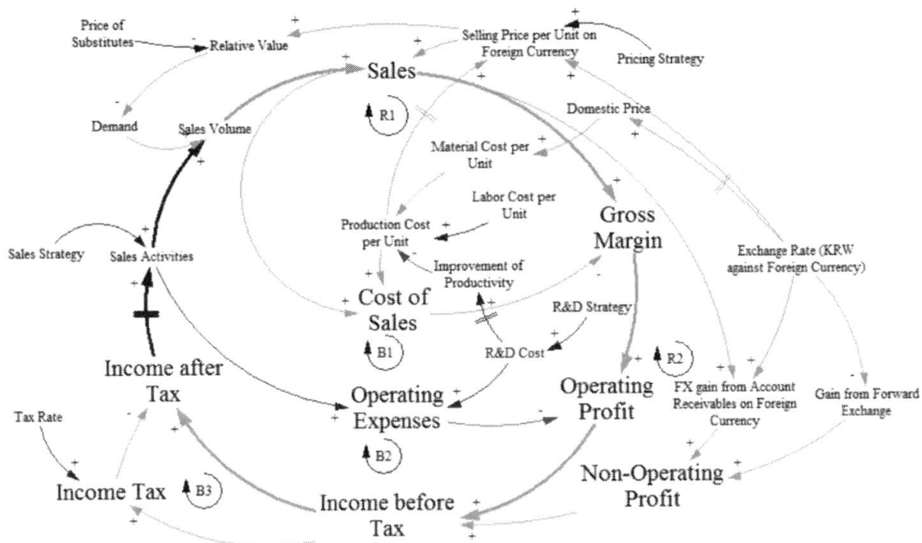

<Figure 7> Example of the causal loop diagram based on financial strategy

<Table 5> Causal relationship based on financial strategy

Reference	Cause and Effect Relationship	Subject of Research	Object of Research
Roh, J., Yun, W., & Kim, S., (1998)	Exchange Rate -> Material, Production output prices(+)	International Hedging Under Concurrent Risks of Input / Output Prices and Exchange Rate : The Case of Korean Oil Refinery	The weekly data of Oil Firms during 1991~1996
Yun, C. (1998)	Product -> Derivative(+)	Study of Exchange Risk Management with Futures and Option	Demand for Futures and Option under Expected Utility
Chung, T., & Lee, K. (2000)	Debt Rate of Foreign Currency, Export -> FX Gain(+), Foreign Exchange Risk Management -> Perfomanace (+)	Foreign Exchange Risk Management Strategy of Korean Firms	113 cases from 670 of Questionnaire
Kim, G., & Jeon, J. (2001)	FX Fluctuation-> Company Value(-) Sales amount, Cost of Sales Change(+) -> Manufacturing Strategy, Marketing Strategy, Financial Strategy(+)	Study of Economic Measurement and Management on Foreign Exchange Exposure for Manufacturing Companies	Manufacturing Companies During 3 years
Yi, C. (2001a)	Foreign Asset Rate -> Derivative Rate(+), Gross Margin Rate -> Derivative Amount(-) FX Gain Rate -> Derivative Amount(+), Export Amount Rate -> Devivative Amount Rate(+)	Analysis of Determinants of Hedge on Foreign Exchange Exposure of Companies from Export and Overseas Investment	ROA, FX Gain and Gross margin for Non-Financial firms listed on KRX between 1999 and 2001

Yi, C. (2001b)	Exchange Risk -> FX Hedging(+)	Measurement and Hedging of Foreign Exchange Risk of Export and Import	Statistics Korea, IFS, KOTIS between 1986 and 2001
Kim, J., & Ban, H. (2002)	Sales to Overseas Rate, Foreign Currency Liability -> Foreign Exchange Exposure(+) -> Derivative(+), Geographic Diversification -> Derivative(-)	The Determinants of Hedging through Derivatives	Non-Financial firms listed on KRX between 1999 and 2000
Yun, C. (2003)	Foreign Exchange Exposure -> Derivative(+), Exchange Risk Management(+)	Study on Management of Effective Exchange Risk with Derivatives	Mean Variance and Utility Function
Yi, C. (2003)	FX Gain -> Derivative(+), Export Ratio -> Derivative(+), Foregin Currency Liability -> Derivative(+)	Foreign Exchange Exposure and Hedging Determinant of Derivatives of International Transaction Firms	ROA, FX Gain, Gross Margin on Non-Financial firms listed on KRX between 1999 and 2001
Kwon, T., & Joo, K. (2004)	Import Ratio -> Foreign Exchange Exposure(+), Foreign Currency Liability -> Foreign Exchange Exposure(+), Foreign Exchange Exposure -> Exchange Risk Management System, FX Insurance, Institutional Support from Government(+)	Foreign Exchange Exposure and Risk Management of Firms in the Yosu National Industrial Complex	8 Companies on Yeosu Industrial Complex, which were listed on KRX between 1990 and 2000
Oh, M. (2004)	Exchange Risk -> Company Value(-)	A Practical Study on the Exchange Risk Management of Shipping Companies	Financial Statements on Shipping Companies During 5 years
Yi, C. (2004b)	FX Fluctuation -> Export Exchange Risk(+) -> Hedging(+)	Foreign Exchange Exposure and Hedging of Trade and Foreign Direct Investment Firms in Busan Area	Busan`s monthly export data for the period 1988-2002 and annual foreign direct investment data for period 1980-2002
Kwon, T. (2006b)	Exchange Risk -> Exchange Risk Management(+)	The Exchange Exposure and the Maximum Exchange Loss in Exchange Risk Analysis	Non-Financial firms listed on KRX between 1990 and 1997
Ban, H., & Kim, S. (2006)	Foreign Exchange Exposure -> Derivative(+)	Interaction Effect of Hedging Strategy on Korean Companies	108 Companies using Derivative, which were Non-Financial firms listed on KRX between 1999 and 2001
Jung, S., & Kwon, T. (2007)	Foreign Currency Liability -> Foreign Exchange Exposure(+) -> Currency Derivative Trading(+) -> Company Value(+)	Does the Use of Foreign Currency Derivatives in Korean Firms Reduce the Exchange Rate Exposure?	Non-Financial firms listed on KRX between 2001 and 2005
Park, S., Kim, H., & Bahng, D. (2009)	Export Ratio -> Exchange Risk(+), Netting -> Exchange Risk(-), Multinational Corporation -> Exchange Risk(+), Derivative -> Exchange Risk Exposure(-), Non-current Asset -> Exchange Risk(-), Lagged Effect of FX	Netting and Hedging Effect on the Exchange Risk Exposure of the Korean Export Firms	213 of Export Companies which were Non-Financial firms listed on KRX between 1997 and 2007
Kwon, T., Chang, U., & Jung, S. (2010)	Export -> Forward Trading(+), Currency Option Trading(+) -> Foreign Exchange Exposure(-),	The Usage of Curruency Derivatives of the Korean Firms and their Management of the Foreign Exchange Rate Exposure	the firms using currency forwards and currency options among the listed firms in KOSPI and KOSDAQ during the period from 2004 to 2008
Kwon, T., & Jung, S. (2010)	Forward Trading, Currency Forward Trading -> Foreign Exchange Exposure(-)	Effects to Asymmetric Foreign Exchange Exposure from Forward Trading and Currency Forward Trading	Non-Financial firms listed on Korea Exchange between 2000 and 2006
Song, H., & Han, S. (2010)	FX Hedge -> Company Value(+)	Testing the Valuation Effect of Foreign Exchange Risk Insurance in Korea	2,857 Companies using FX related Insurance, which were listed on KRX and registered on KOSDAQ between 2000 and 2008
Kwon, T., Park, R., & Bea, S. (2011a)	Debt Ratio, Firm Size, Export Ratio -> Derivative(+)	Derivatives Use, Firm Value, Risk and Determinants: Evidence of Korean Firms	Non-Financial firms listed on Korea Exchange between 2000 and 2008
Kwon, T., Park, R., & Bea, S. (2011b)	Forward Selling Trading, Trading with the Related Company on Overseas, Capital Finance of Foreign Currency -> Foreign Exchange Exposure(-), Price Passthrough -> Foreign Exchange Exposure(-)	On the Effectiveness of Foreign Exchange Rate Exposure Hedging with Derivatives for Korean Industrial Companies	Non-Financial firms listed on Korea Exchange between 2007 and 2009

3.2.2 The causal loop diagram on operational strategy

Operational strategy may be understood as various strategies that cannot be classified as either financial or pricing strategy. <Table 6> shows the related papers. Chung (2001) mentioned that regarding the foreign currency exposure management of Korean automakers, they might decrease the drop in enterprise value caused by foreign currency exposure through increasing the market share. Kim (2002) argued that dominating the market might decrease the risk relevant to exchange rate fluctuation because it might increase the enterprise value. Gwag et al. (2003) mentioned that overseas raw material supply and overseas direct investment might alleviate the foreign currency exposure. Kwon (2009) explained that business diversification might alleviate the foreign currency exposure. Kim (2011) stated that the companies might alleviate the foreign currency exposure through product differentiation, R&D, etc. Kwak (2012) mentioned that through the effect from exchange rate fluctuation to investment, the companies with dominant power over the market might decrease the foreign currency exposure. Jeong & Chung (2012) proved that the share of the investment from foreigners affected the foreign currency exposure.

<Figure 8> is the map on the causal relationship of the operational strategy. Operational strategy is an effort to decrease the company's foreign currency exposure over the long-term. In case the operating profit decreases due to increase in the purchase price caused by the increase in the exchange rate, purchase price may be decreased through operational strategy. The table shows the decrease in purchase price through the investment in overseas factories and the drop in production cost by improving productivity based on R&D strategies. In addition, the consequent decrease in the foreign currency exposure through product differentiation may also be considered. This book considered the causal loop diagram

on the occasion where the companies that were classified as type A, which was the most common type, invested in overseas factories and where the R&D strategies were implemented. In case the exchange rate increases, purchase price increases, and, as a result, the needs for operational strategy increase. In case the overseas factory is established, purchase price may decrease. In other words, it is to hedge against the damage caused by the increase in purchase price affected by the exchange rate increase through decreasing the purchase price by producing goods in overseas factory. In addition, if the business size increases, operating expenses may decrease through enhancing efficiency in operation over the long-term. Also, when making investment in R&D, production cost may constantly decrease through productivity enhancement, and corporate profit may increase over the long-term. Various operational strategies offset against the negative impact from exchange rate to gross margin and operating profit and may improve the company's profit in a constant manner.

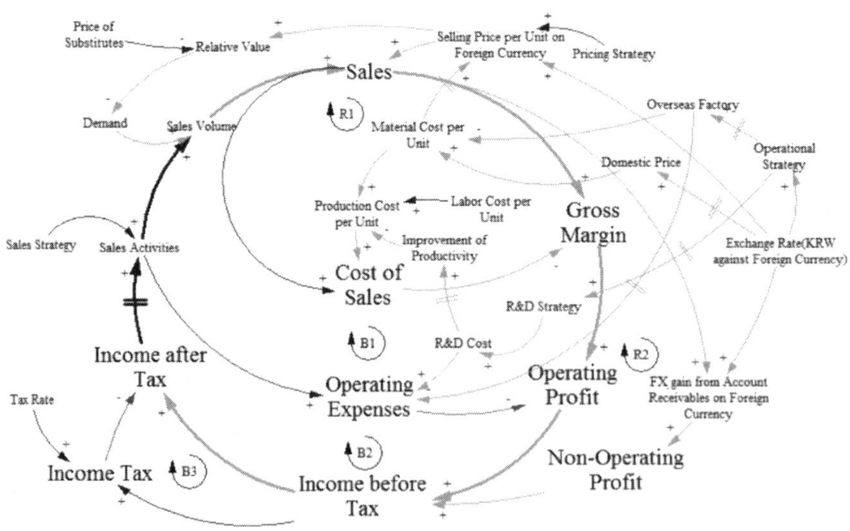

<Figure 8> Example of the causal loop diagram based on operational strategy

<Table 6> Causal relationship based on operational strategy

Reference	Cause and Effect Relationship	Subject of Research	Object of Research
Chung, C. (2001)	Foreign Exchange Exposure-> Export(-)-> Market Share(-)-> Company Value(-)	Foreign Exchange Exposure Management of the Korean Automobile Companies	Auto Companies listed on KRX between 1987 and 1997
Kim, H. (2002a)	Monopoly of Market -> Company Value(+)	Exchange Rates and Market Power: Alternative Measure of Residual Demand	the monthly data over January 1991-March 2001 for Export
Gwag, T., Jeong, C., Sin, S., & Choe, S. (2003)	Export -> Exchange Risk(+), Foreign Currency Debt -> Exchange Risk(+), Procurement of Materials from Overseas, Foreign Currency Debt, Direct Investment to Overseas -> Exchange Risk from Export(-), Structure of Competition - Exchange Risk from Export(-)	A Study on the Foreign Exchange Exposure of Korean Exporting Companies	Manufacturing Companies listed on KRX between 1995 and 2001, which had over 10% of Export Ration
Shin, S. (2003)	Foreign Exchange Exposure -> Corporate Investment(-)	The Impact of Capital Market Imperfections and Exchange Rate Uncertainty on Corporate Investment	353 Manufacturing Companies listed on KRX between 1982 and 1996
Lee, Y., Choe, J, & Kim, D. (2008)	FX Fluctuation -> Corporate Investment	An Economic Analysis for Effect of Exchange Rate Fluctuation to Corporate Investment	Non-Financial firms listed on KRX between 1990 and 2006
Kwon, T. (2009)	Trading between Intercompanies -> Foreign Exchange Exposure(-) Foreign Exchange Exposure->Diversification of Companies(+)	Internal Transactions within Business Group and Management of Foreign Exchange Exposure	Non-Financial firms listed on KRX between 2000 and 2006
Kim, S. (2011)	Diversification of Geographical Strategy -> Foreign Exchange Exposure(+), Strategy of Product Differentiation -> Foreign Exchange Exposure(+), R&D -> Foreign Exchange Exposure(-)	The effect of the interaction between FDI Location and product differentiation on the foreign exchange exposure	Non-Financial firms listed on KRX between 2002 and 2006, which had subsidiary company
Kwak, T. (2012)	Large Company, Export Company, Hedging FX Risk -> Investment(+), Market Dominating Power -> Exchange Risk(-)	International Economics : The Effects of the Exchange Rate on Investment	Korean manufacturing firms using firm-level panel data during the period between 1990 and 2010
Jeong, Y., & Chung, H. (2012)	FX Fluctuation -> Stock Price Earnings(-), Lagging FX Fluctuation -> Stock Price Earnings(-), Foreign Investment Ratio -> Foreign Exchange Exposure(+)	Foreign exchange exposure of Korean firms and its relationship with foreign investors` investment	Monthly Earnings Data of Companies listed on KRX between 1990 and 2006

3.2.3 The causal loop diagram on pricing strategy

Pricing strategy is to transfer the risk to the customers because according to the strategy, exporters increase the sales price to preserve the gross margin in case either the sales price decreases or the purchase price increases due to change in the exchange rate. <Table 7> shows the related papers. Kwon & Hwang (1999) stated that in case the import price increased, companies marked up the export price. Kwon & Joo (2002) mentioned that the pricing could be done to manage the foreign currency risk. Some researchers (Kim, 2002b; Kwak, 2004; Lee & Lee, 2004) carried out the empirical study on the pricing actions caused by the fluctuation in the exchange rate. Park & Chung (2006) explained that the small- and mid-sized exporters carried out pricing strategy for foreign currency management. Choi & Ham (2013) discovered that depending on the share in the overseas market, level of product differentiation, and level of capital intensity, pricing was done in a different manner.

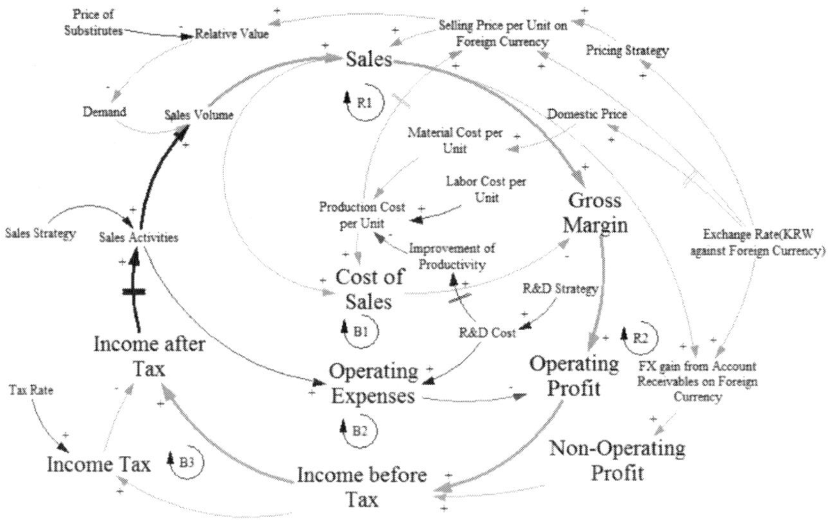

<Figure 9> Example of the causal loop diagram based on pricing strategy

<Figure 9> is the causal loop diagram representing the causal relationships explained by the papers. In case the purchase price increases due to exchange rate, companies increase the sales price through pricing in order to respond to the decrease in the operating profit caused by the increase in the purchase price. As a result, operating profit increases, and the income may be maintained at a certain level. However, in the case of overseas sales, the increase in exchange rate directly elevates the sales price, and the companies would not consider pricing actions. However, in case the exchange rate decreases, the sales price drops. If the purchase price does not change, the gross margin will decrease. The com-

panies will consider taking pricing actions. In the case of type C companies, they would consider the sales price in pricing strategy because the purchase price goes up when the exchange rate increases. Therefore, there should be understanding of different corporate types in pricing strategies.

<Table 7> Example of the causal loop diagram based on pricing strategy

Reference	Cause and Effect Relationship	Subject of Research	Object of Research
Kwon, T., & Hwang, H. (1999a)	Import -> Export Mark-up(+)	Analysis of Characteristics of Mark-up Adjustment from FX Fluctuation on Export Industry in Korea	Export Data of Korea Foreign Trade Association between 1991 and 1999
Kwon, T. (2001)	FX Fluctuation -> Price Passthrough(+)	Exchange Rate Change and Markup Adjustment of Major Korean Exports during Korea`s Foreign Currency Crisis	Manufacturing Companies listed on KRX between 1996 and 2000
Kwon, T., & Joo, K. (2002)	Export -> Exchange Risk(+), Foreign Currency Debt -> Exchange Risk(+), Procurement of Materials from Overseas, Foreign Currency Debt, Direct Investment to Overseas -> Exchange Risk from Export(-), Structure of Competition - Exchange Risk from Export(-)	Determinants of Mark - up Adjustment According to the Exchange Rate Change in Korea's Major Exports	Analysis of Domestic Companies between 1996 and 2000
Kim, H. (2002b)	FX Fluctuation -> Export Price(+)	The Pricing-to-Market Effects of Exchange Rate with Residual Demand	Monthly Data of Export over January 1990-March 2001
Kwak, T. (2004)	FX Fluctuation -> Price Passthrough(+)	Exchange Rate Pass-Through and Import Prices in Korea's Manufacturing Industries	Manufacturing Companies listed on KRX between 1980 and 2001
Lee, K., & Lee, M. (2004)	Trading between Intercompanies -> Foreign Exchange Exposure(-) Foreign Exchange Exposure->Diversification of Companies(+)	Exchange Rate Variability and Pricing Behavior of Korean Firms: the Mark-up Response in Industry Level	16 Manufacturing Companies between 1980 and 2000
Park, J., & Cheong, J. (2006)	Diversification of Geographical Strategy -> Foreign Exchange Exposure(+), Strategy of Product Differentiation -> Foreign Exchange Exposure(+), R&D -> Foreign Exchange Exposure(-)	Study on Countermeasure of Export Small and Medium Sized Companies from FX fluctuation	Survey of 407 Export Companies on 2005
Kwon, T., & Joo, K. (2011)	Large Company, Export Company, Hedging FX Risk -> Investment(+), Market Dominating Power -> Exchange Risk(-)	A Study on the Expected and Observed Exchange Rate Exposure of Korean Firms	Non-Financial firms listed on KRX between 2004 and 2008
Choi, C., & Ham, H. (20013)	FX Fluctuation -> Stock Price Earnings(-), Lagging FX Fluctuation -> Stock Price Earnings(-), Foreign Investment Ratio -> Foreign Exchange Exposure(+)	An Analysis on the pass-through on Korean export prices of Exchange rate changes	Export Price of Korea, Price of Competing Country, FX Rate on Competing Country, Producer Price Index of Korea, Exchange Rate of Won, USA Business Barometer, Data from Bank of Korea between 2008 and 2011

3.2.4 Consideration of strategies depending on the fluctuation of exchange rate

The aforementioned three strategies consider both the increase and decrease in exchange rate. The impact from the increase and decrease in exchange rate are different. Considering this asymmetry, this book will aim to confirm the impact from the elevation and drop in the exchange rate and review the adequate strategies. Over the long-term, the impact from the exchange rate may be offset due to the impact from multiple variables. To take a look at the impact from the increase and decrease in exchange rate, this book separated the impact from type A companies' short-term exposure to foreign currency into <Figure 10> and <Figure 11>. In <Figure 10>, type A companies' net income increases over the short-term, once the exchange rate increases. However, as shown in <Figure 11>, the companies' net income decreases, once the exchange rate drops. In case these companies use hedging through getting involved in the forward contract as part of their financial strategy, the causal loop diagram in <Figure 12> and <Figure 13> may be considered. In <Figure 12>, once the exchange rate increases, net income increases without any strategy. However, in case they use financial strategy, the non-operating profit decreases, and the increase in operating profit is offset in earning before tax. In <Figure 13>, the financial strategy against the possibility where the exchange rate drops to decrease the gross margin is found. It becomes a hedging strategy to offset the decrease in earnings before tax through increasing the value of the forward product. Some managements believe that strategies are meaningless, since in case the exchange rate increases, it brings profit to the company, while it causes damage when it decreases. In addition, they purchase forward products when it seems that the exchange rate would decrease, while maintaining status quo when it seems that the rate would increase. However, the fluctuation of exchange rate is so complex that its increase and decrease cannot be expected. That is why they cannot generate profit through hedging. Hedging is meaningful because the enterprise value is preserved through offset. However, since the operational strategy is the one to expand the corporate profit in a fundamental manner, it should be considered regardless of the increase and decrease in the exchange rate. Therefore, as part of the strategy to alleviate the foreign currency exposure, companies should establish the financial, pricing, and operational strategy in a comprehensive manner.

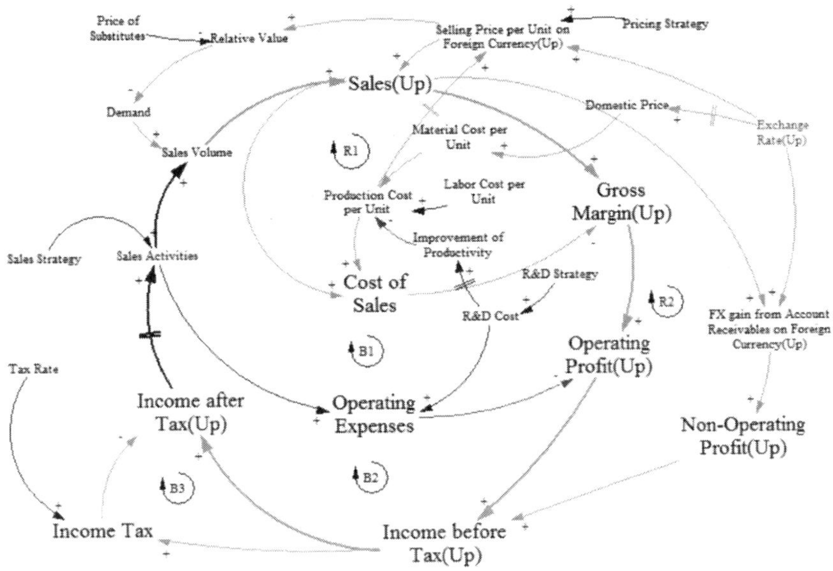

<Figure 10> Example of the causal loop diagram based on the increase in exchange rate

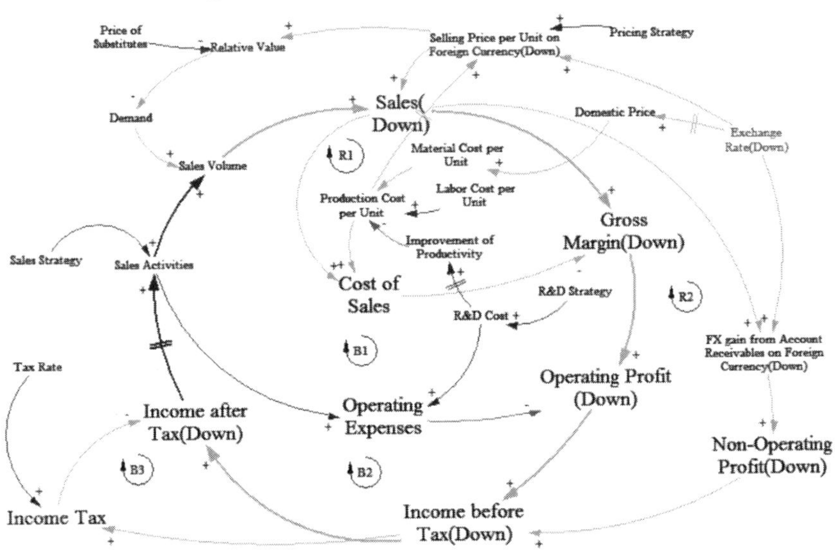

<Figure 11> Example of the causal loop diagram on the decrease in exchange rate

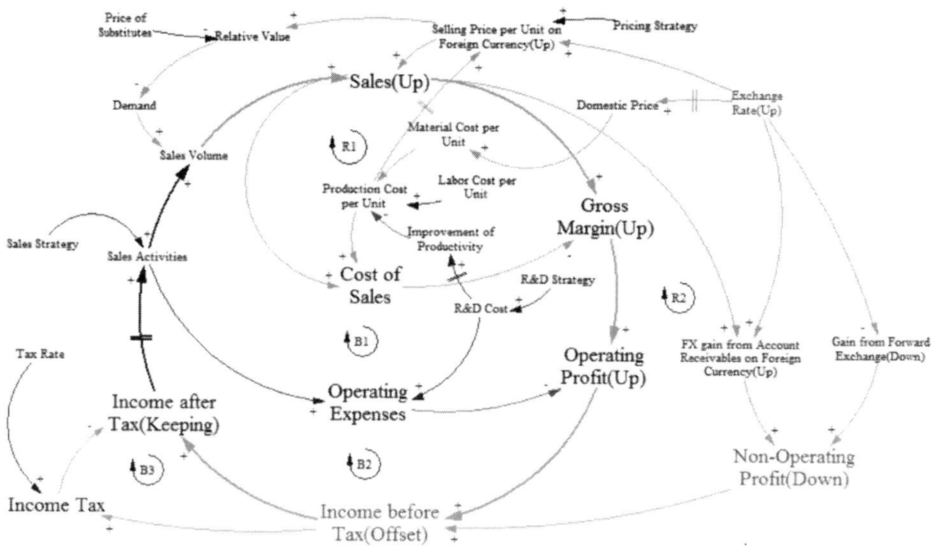

<Figure 12> Example of the causal loop diagram based on financial strategy to respond to the increase in exchange rate

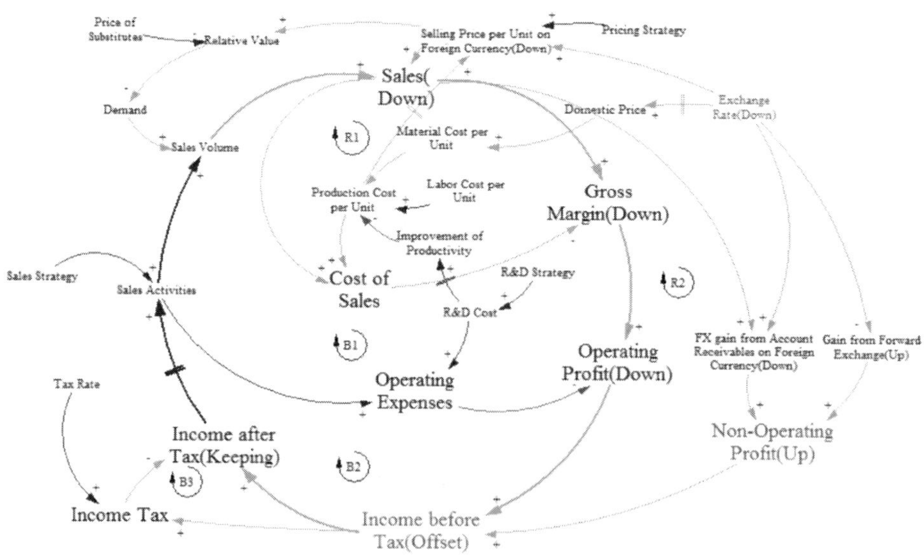

<Figure 13> Example of the causal loop diagram based on financial strategy to respond to the decrease in exchange rate

3.3 Building of the integrated causal loop diagram

In the previous chapter, the strategies to alleviate the foreign currency exposure were explained based on the case of type A companies. However, companies may use complex strategy to alleviate the foreign currency exposure, instead of using a single strategy because depending on the corporate type, even the same strategy to alleviate the foreign currency exposure may have different effect. Based on the aforementioned causal loop diagram, the comprehensive causal relationship may be drawn for each type and strategy as shown in <Figure 14>, <Figure 15>, <Figure 16>, and <Figure 17>. Companies are constantly affected by the factors that determine foreign currency exposure, and various strategic approaches may be taken against such factors. Since the factors that determine foreign currency exposure derive from corporate structure, one strategy alone cannot be sufficient. Financial strategy hedges against the decrease in enterprise value due to foreign currency exposure through directly affecting the value of the forward product. However, operational and pricing strategy are to decrease the foreign currency exposure through adjusting the factors inside the company that affect the exposure.

If you take a look at each corporate type, you may see that the impact from each strategy is different. Companies use the strategy to alleviate the foreign currency exposure in a complex manner. However, depending on the corporate type, there are strategic differences. <Figure 14> indicates the strategy to alleviate the foreign currency exposure of the companies that sell overseas and buy locally. Through financial strategy, it hedges against the loss caused by the change in the exchange rate that affects net income through non-operating profit. In addition, through operational strategy, it may decrease the effect on local price (+), purchase price (+) and production cost (+) with the decrease in the purchase price (-) enabled by overseas factories. The pricing strategy against the exchange rate effect shows that sales (+), operating profit (+), and net income (+) may be secured through increasing sales price (+), transferring the impact from the increase in the local price (+) and purchase price (+).

<Figure 15> indicates the case where the sales and purchase occur overseas. Since the sales and purchase are simultaneously made in foreign currency, the size of the foreign currency exposure is not so large. However, since the transaction only takes place in foreign currency, there is impact from the exchange rate. Regarding this type, even though operational strategy helps, the loss caused by the time gap between the sales and purchase could be hedged through forward products, and through pricing strategy, the decrease in gross margin (-) caused by the decrease in the exchange rate may be hedged.

<Figure 16> indicates the case where both the sales and purchase occur locally, and therefore, the change in the exchange rate is not immediately reflected. However, since there is impact from the local price (+) over the long-term, companies may consider pricing strategy. Operational strategy may help; however, this cannot be considered as a strategy solely for exchange rate, and it seems that there is no need to consider forward products.

<Figure 17> indicates the cases where sales occur locally, while purchase takes place overseas. Since the change in the exchange rate is directly reflected on the purchase price (+) and impacts the cost of sales (+) and gross margin (-), companies may carry out hedging for operating profit (-) through forward products and through transferring the impact from the increase in purchase price to sales price (+) and sales (+), they may preserve operating profit (+).

The part of each strategy that should be strengthened differs by type. In addition, since asymmetry exists in foreign currency exposure between companies

(Yi 2001a; Kwon 2007), the size of the impact from exchange rate should be understood. It seems that the companies that sell overseas and buy locally do not need a strategy because if the exchange rate decreases, the foreign currency exposure increases, while the exposure decreases, and operating profit increases, once the rate increases. On the contrary, it seems that the companies that sell locally and buy overseas do not need a strategy because if the exchange rate increases, the foreign currency exposure increases, while the operating profit decreases, once the rate decreases. However, it is impossible to predict the increase and decrease of exchange rate. In addition, since the indirect impact exists due to time gap, all companies need double strategies to prepare themselves against the time when the rate increases and decreases. Management should not make a decision to increase the company's exposure to foreign currency by having faith in either increase or decrease of the exchange rate.

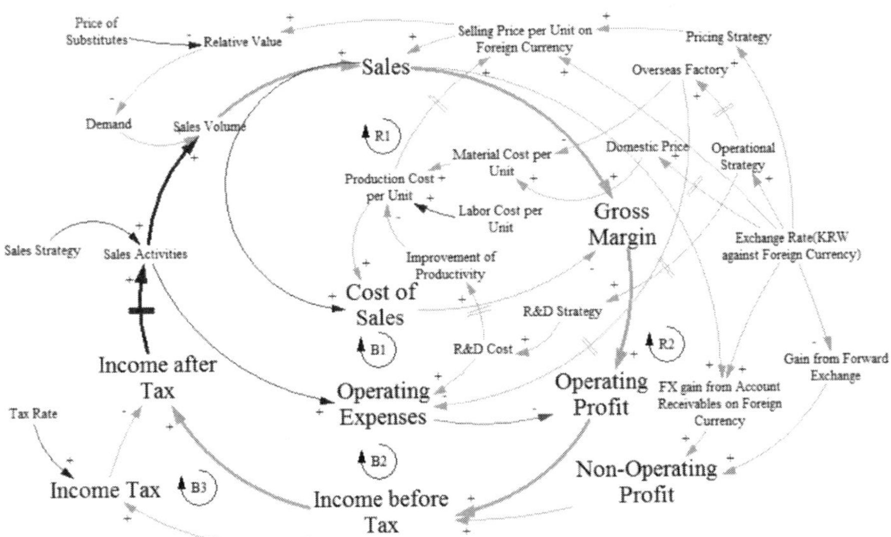

<Figure 14> Comprehensive causal loop diagram on type A

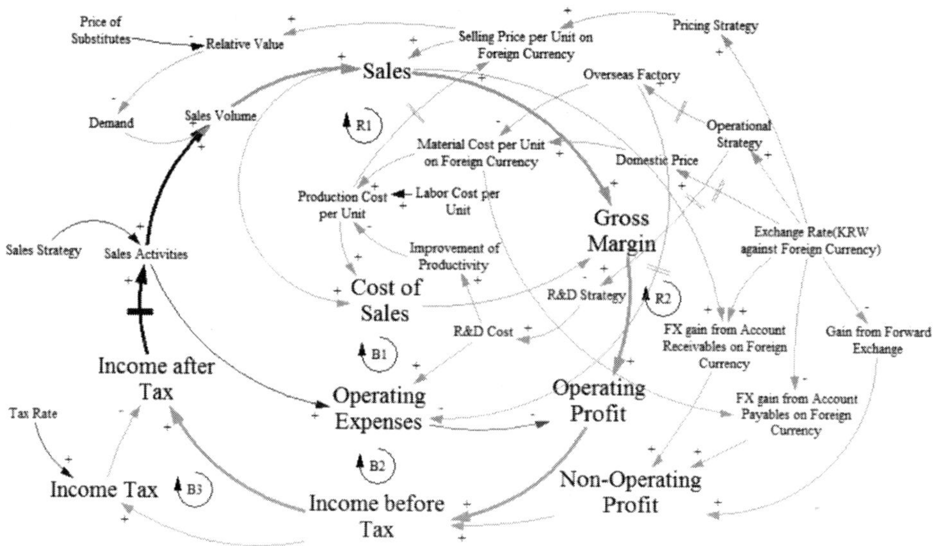

<Figure 15> Comprehensive causal loop diagram on type B

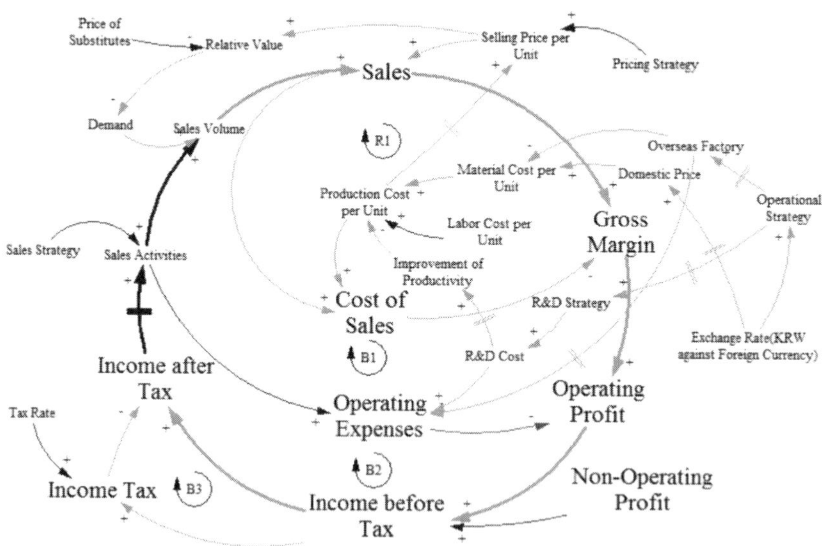

<Figure 16> Comprehensive causal loop diagram on type C

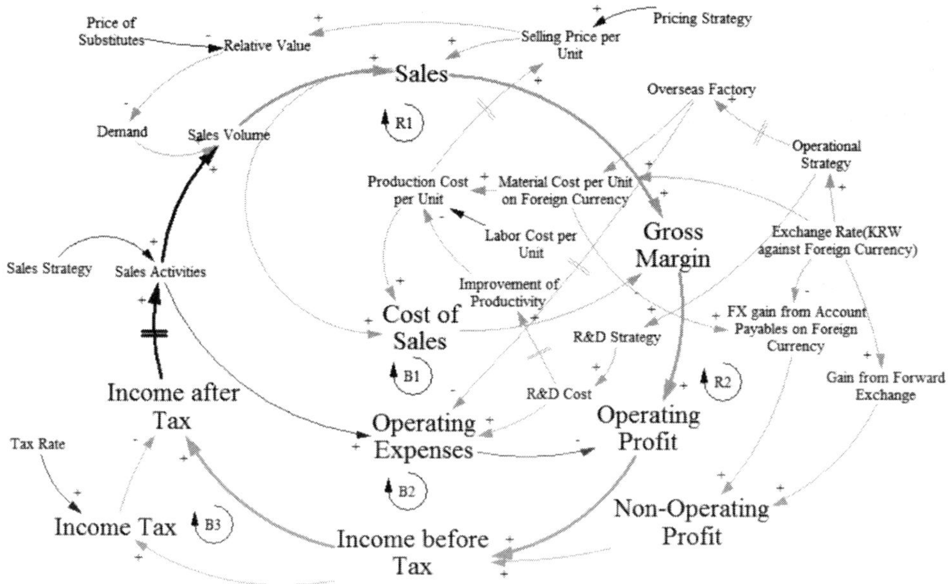

<Figure 17> Comprehensive causal loop diagram on type D

4. Conclusion

4.1 Summary and implication

While the previous studies could not understand the dynamic flow of the exchange rate fluctuation in business management because they carried out simple and static researches, this book summarized the causal relationship among various factors through summing up and classifying the previous research results. Through this, the various paths of the exchange rate fluctuation and business management could be understood in a comprehensive manner. The lessons from this research may be summarized as follows:

Firstly, the corporate activity causal loop diagram based on income statement may help the readers easily understand and approach the structure of system dynamics. It is believed that they would have no difficulties in understanding the causal loop diagram based on income statement, if they have understanding of financial statements. In addition, it could be easily confirmed through this causal loop diagram that the exchange rate fluctuation affects all parts of companies' financial statements.

Secondly, this research discovers that the factors in companies to determine the foreign currency exposure and the strategy to alleviate the exposure affected each other and gave feedbacks to the change in the enterprise value. This research shows that companies' complex sales activities and the strategy to alleviate the foreign currency exposure work dynamically with the internal mechanism to have complex impact on net income. In addition, it showed a loop where net income enhances the sales activities to increase the sales.

Thirdly, this book showed that in Korea that is highly dependent on the global economic system and export, it is efficient for the companies to preserve their value by responding to foreign currency exposure through the strategy to alleviate the foreign currency exposure. Companies have their own factors to determine foreign currency exposure, depending on their activities and should strive to find a strategy that suits their type. Depending on their type, each company should understand the factors that determine foreign currency exposure and establish the financial, operational, and pricing strategy, accordingly. However, since the previous studies were focused more on simple analysis, they have limitation in introducing a comprehensive strategy. Therefore, there are many companies that respond passively to the change in the exchange rate without having the exchange rate strategy. This research tried to explain the foreign currency exposure and the strategy to alleviate the exposure through the causal loop diagram of system dynamics. In this respect, I think this research would help the companies to easily understand the foreign currency exposure and establish the responses in an active manner.

Fourthly, this book took a separate look at the impact from strategy on exchange rate increase and decrease. However, since it is impossible to predict the increase and decrease in exchange rate due to its excessive volatility, this book discovered that it was more effective to propose the foreign currency exposure and the strategy to alleviate the exposure for each type in a comprehensive manner. The comprehensive causal loop diagram for each type will help the companies understand and analyze the strategy to alleviate the foreign currency exposure. This will help comprehensive understanding of the previous researches and preparation of the comprehensive strategy to alleviate the foreign currency exposure based on the proposed causal relationships. In particular, it was confirmed that the operational strategy is effective over the long-term, regardless of the increase and decrease in exchange rate.

Fifthly, this book analyzed the various paths through which the exchange rate affects the business management and the responses to this by utilizing the causal loop diagram. Without systematic thinking, companies have no other option but to take a simple approach against the foreign currency exposure and to have the financial strategy as the only strategy to alleviate the foreign currency exposure. This book explained that if one takes a look at the foreign currency exposure with systematic mindset, they would consider various operational strategies. It was shown that investment in overseas factories and productivity enhancement through R&D strategies might offset the impact from the foreign currency exposure and increase profit for the companies, even though it took some time.

Even though the research method to sum up the complicated causal relationship from the previous studies to come up with the causal loop diagram on the circular causal relationship has been recently introduced (Chung & Lee, 2012), this book has made the first attempt to understand the foreign currency exposure and is expected to lay ground for the future studies to analyze foreign currency exposure and the strategy to alleviate the exposure based on system dynamics thinking.

4.2 Limitation

Based on system dynamics thinking, this research proposed the comprehensive causal loop diagram on companies' strategy to alleviate the foreign currency exposure. After dividing the companies into four types, this book understood the dynamic flows caused by exchange rate fluctuation in each type. However, each company may qualify for multiple corporate types. The complex causal loop diagram may be drawn based on such cases. However, the discussion may become too complicated and distracting. This book was focused on introducing the systematic structure of foreign currency exposure and the strategy to alleviate the exposure based on each type and strategy. The detailed research on the complex causal loop diagram on the abovementioned cases should be followed up.

In addition, the approach taken by this book helps the comprehensive understanding of foreign currency exposure and the strategy to alleviate the exposure. However, it has limitation in providing the micro-explanation on the strategy to alleviate the foreign currency exposure. The future research to provide the explanation on the various results caused by the interaction between positive and negative feedbacks represented on the causal loop diagram and the solution is required.

IV Application of System Dynamics

1. Purpose and need of the research

The derivatives market in Korea has grown rapidly. <Table 8> shows that domestic financial derivatives trading amounted to 57 quadrillion won in 2013. Considering that the annual budget of the Korean government is 385 trillion won, it is not difficult to imagine how large the market for derivatives is. The securities derivatives are traded through securities companies, normally. However the most of the currency derivatives are traded by banks. As a result, it is no doubt that such a large scale of trading has a significant impact on the domestic economy.

The main reason of purchasing trading derivatives is to hedge their exchange rate risk (Kim & Ban, 2002). As the international trades by domestic companies have grown, the exposure from exchange rate has increased. It is why many companies manage the risk of exchange rate through derivatives. Therefore, the market has recorded rapid growth. Due to the excessive dependency upon foreign markets, many companies have been affected by changes in exchange rate in terms of managerial issues (Kwon & Hwang, 1999b). To hedge this exchange rate risk, most of the companies choose derivatives.

<Table 8> Trading volume of derivatives by financial companies

(Unit: Trillion won, %)

Div		2012	2013	Bank	Securities	Insurance	Trust	Etc
Total		60,564	57,121	12,424	42,950	101	692	954
Stock		40,988	37,456	83	36,879	25	153	316
	Derivatives Option	40,825	37,334	58	36,786	21	153	316
Interest Rate		9,203	9,634	3,605	5,352	32	152	493
	Interest rate SWAP	2,320	2,588	2,199	385	1	2	1
Currency		10,307	9,957	8,721	668	43	381	144
	Forward Exchange	9,107	8,695	8,089	252	26	322	6
Credit		28	41	3	37	1	0	0
	CDS	21	33	3	30	0	0	0
Etc		38	33	12	14	0	6	1

Source : Financial Supervisory Service on April 2nd, 2014

The economic crisis triggered by sub-prime mortgages from the United States in 2008 had a huge impact on the Korean economy (Kim & Kim, 2009). The roller-coaster fluctuation of macroeconomic variables such as exchange rate, stock prices, and interest rate drove the domestic economy into confusion. Particularly, due to a sudden spike in the exchange rate, many small and medium-sized companies were suffering for years. The companies that purchased KIKO (Knock-In Knock-Out) option faced a huge amount of foreign exchange losses. KIKO option is one of the derivatives that was used by many exports companies to manage exchange rate risk in a time when the exchange rate was stable before 2008 (Kim & Jun, 2012). It was developed to manage the risk caused by changes in exchange rate when the exchange rate was in a stabilizing trend. It was a financial product derived from forward exchange. KIKO has one of the inherent risks that derivatives have. Nevertheless, many companies overlooked the risks, and bought it only with the view of favorable aspects. Financial institutions also advertised favorable conditions (Kim & Jun, 2012).

However, exchange rate changes have a hard-to-predict volatility (Kwon & Hwang, 1999b). As the changes in exchange rate fluctuated from the financial meltdown, KIKO caused tremendous losses for companies. Losses of domestic companies reached 3 trillion and 200 billion won, and the related lawsuits are still ongoing despite the ruling by the Supreme Court in September 2013 (E-Today, April 8th, 2014). The derivatives for managing exchange rate risk became a risky product that greatly increased the risk of exchange rate unintentionally. Companies might misunderstand the structural risk of derivatives. In this study, I analyzed the structure of derivatives using system dynamics, and I found the structural problems of KIKO. Through simulation, I try to confirm the risks involved in the fluctuation of exchange rates.

2. System Dynamics and the Basic Model of Derivatives

2.1 System dynamics in financial market

The more the companies are engaged in sales, the more they are exposed to foreign exchange. That is why they hedge foreign exchange to maintain the value of a company. According to George & Grover (1987), a financial market should be regarded as an organism in which interactions among market participants and expectations are always changing in a dynamic way, rather than a subject of static balance affected by the invisible hand, which they called reflexivity theory. The claim is in line with the systems thinking. In this regard, we adopted systems thinking to explain KIKO since it is originated from the financial market.

2.2 Drawing basic model

A basic model of derivatives was drawn from <Figure 7>, a causal loop diagram of financial strategy suggested on the previous chapter. <Figure 18> is a causal loop diagram of financial strategy that is standard for regular export companies. The reason why companies buy derivatives is to hedge the risks of foreign exchange exposure. Thus, we bring the basic model of derivatives from a causal loop diagram of financial strategy. <Figure 7> shows various activities of companies. It is not easy to determine the causal effect of derivatives due to the impact of net income caused by other factors. The model and simulation were made in this book. <Figure 19> was drawn from <Figure 18>. It shows a simplified causal loop diagram focusing on derivatives to more clearly understand the impact of derivatives. Sales are generated by the sales activities of a company; Account Receivables (AR) are generated from international trades. And, if AR are increased, foreign currency receivables are also increased. To

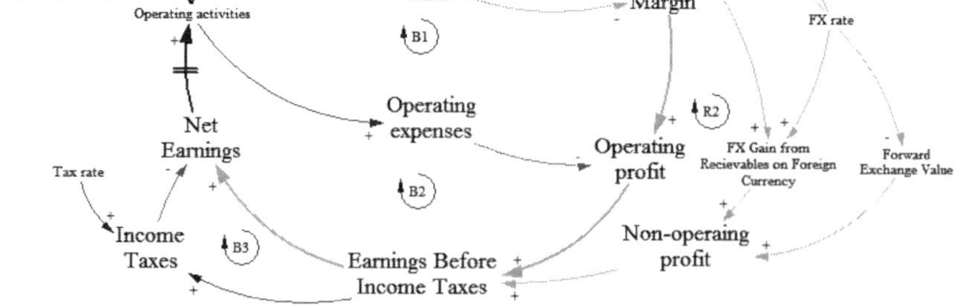

<Figure 18> Causal loop diagram depending on the financial strategy

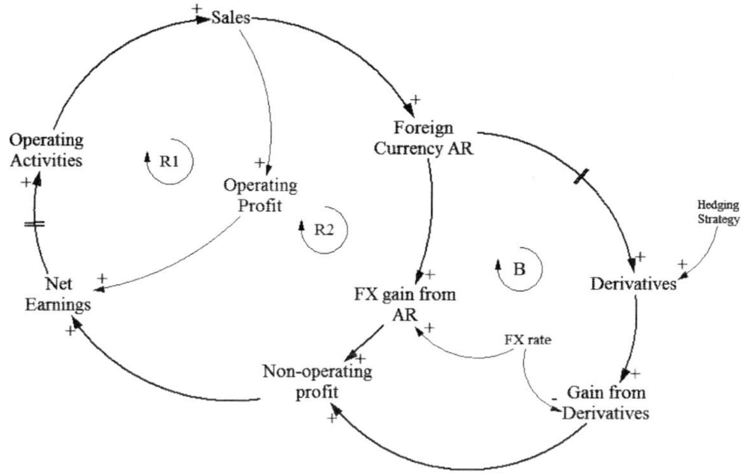

<Figure 19> Simplified causal loop diagram of derivatives

hedge the exchange rate risk against foreign currency receivables, companies normally buy derivatives. There is some delay because of the observation of foreign currency receivables. Derivatives is normally expected not for gain, but for hedge. If FX gains from AR increase, gain from derivatives should decrease because of the purpose of the hedge.

3. Causal loop diagram and simulation for KIKO derivatives

3.1 Structural analysis on KIKO derivatives

KIKO is a currency option contract consisting of "Knock-in" and "Knock-out". It is a currency option combined with put option and call option. Knock-in means that the option becomes effective after a certain point, and Knock-out means that the option becomes invalid if the exchange rate reaches a certain point. In other words, if the exchange rate reaches a pre-contracted point, the contract becomes either knock-out or knock-in. This condition can control the wielding price and dealing price of an option to a level that a client wants. Knock-out condition to a purchasing put option can reduce the scope of hedge and increase the sale price of the call option higher than the purchase price of the put option, which increases the wielding price of the KIKO option. Existing hedging methods such as forward exchange or exchange risk insurance require fees or deposits. These can be accepted as a necessary cost to manage risks. But it would be considered a good change for companies not to pay such costs if possible. There can be a certain amount of foreign-exchange profit, which could be very attractive for companies. If the exchange rate slides into a range that forms knock-in and knock-out, there can be some profit. But, if the exchange rate escape from the range, the company has to bear a huge amount of losses. However, if an export company made a contract within the estimated amount of exports, foreign exchange exposure is minimized since it can have exchange profit in the export amount. In that case, it cannot expect exchange profit in a range, which was why it made a leverage contract exceeding the export amounts. Due to a sudden spike in the exchange rate, foreign exchange loss from KIKO exceeded the exchange profit from exports which led to a significant amount of losses for companies. <Figure 20> well represents the KIKO currency option (Kim et. al., 2012). If a knock-in and knock-out range is set, this range does not have a cost price, and can generate profit. Put option becomes invalid in knock-out range and call option becomes valid in knock-in range. If a company has a KIKO contract only for hedging, it does not generate any particular losses since it offsets them in the sale of the call option. But it seems that companies made a mistake in this point. They overlooked the fact that there can be a low risk only when the exchange rate is stable. While they have a low risk in a stabilized exchange rate, the risk could skyrocket if the exchange rate increases suddenly. To get a zero cost and some profit in knock-in and knock-out, they had to make a contract twice size of put option price. That is why many companies made contracts far exceeding their export amount. <Figure 21> is similar to the causal loop diagram of general derivatives. However, they have a structure of varying the purchase amount of KIKO depending on the certainty of having a profit. KIKO can also act like general derivatives if one purchases KIKO thinking of the function of general derivatives. To have the function of an option, one needs to make a contract twice the size of the put option price, which is why it increases risks if you try to have a profit from KIKO. We can see delay effect on R1 and B loop. If a company get good net income, CEO decides to strengthen operating activities to get more net income. As a result, after a company finds out what foreign currency AR increase, it increases KIKO.

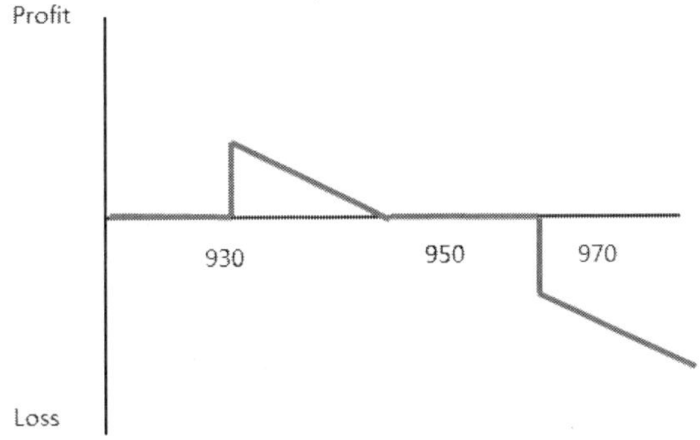

<Figure 20> Profit and loss structure of KIKO by each section (Kim & Kim, 2009)

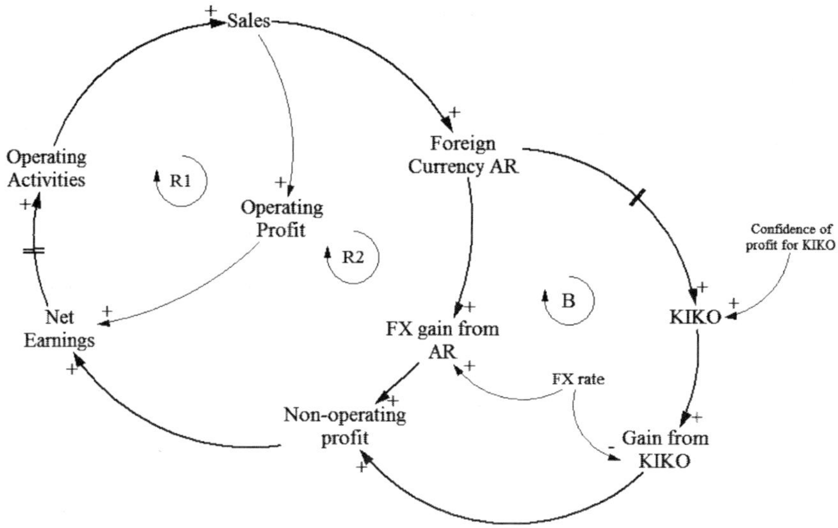

<Figure 21> Causal loop diagram of KIKO derivatives

3.2 Financial crisis and KIKO derivatives

The world financial crisis that started from the sub-prime mortgage crisis in the United States in 2008 instantly changed the atmosphere of the world economy and dealt a major blow to the Korean economy (Kim & Kim, 2009). Many companies had not forecasted the financial crisis.

<Table 9> suggests that there were no big fluctuations in the exchange rate from 2003 to 2008. The fluctuation got a sudden increase in the exchange rate after May 2008. The monthly change was more than 200 won. The fluctuation was stabilized in around January 2011. <Table 10> shows how much loss companies had suffering from KIKO due to the exchange rate fluctuation caused by the economic shock. Consequently, KIKO caused a significant amount of losses, 3,2 trillion won in total; 2.3 trillion won of which was from small and medium-sized companies. This suggests that how inexperienced those small and

medium-sized companies were with FX hedging. Financial institutions that sold KIKO did not give a sufficient explanation of the risks. After all, companies suffered from losses and filed lawsuits against banks. Many small and medium-sized companies were enraged at financial institutions that had sold KIKO as if it had no risks. As of April 2014, there are still lawsuits, and indirect damages from KIKO would reach 1 trillion won (Edaily, April 2nd, 2004). <Table 11> presents the list of lawsuits (Kim & Jun, 2012) Many companies suffered from material loss due to KIKO and filed lawsuits. Still, lawsuits have not been closed. That means that there were significant aftereffects. Most of the cases were ruled that financial institutions had not fulfilled their responsibility.

<Table 9> Yearly changes in FX rate (unit: won)

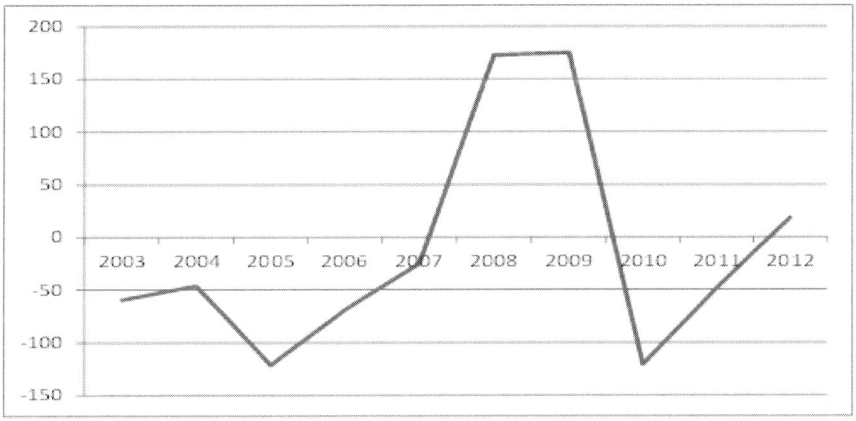

<Table 10> Losses of companies that made KIKO contracts

Division	Realized gain and loss (₩ 100 mil)			Non-realized gain and loss (₩ 100 mil)			Total gain and loss (= realized + non-realized) (₩ 100 mil)		
	Dec. 31st. 2008	Dec. 31st. 2009	Dec. 31st. 2010	Dec. 31st. 2008	Dec. 31st. 2009	Dec. 31st. 2010	Dec. 31st. 2008	Dec. 31st. 2009	Dec. 31st. 2010
Small and Medium-sized companies	-14,970	-21,935	-22,582	-8,842	-1,459	-678	-23,812	-23,394	-23,260
Large corporations	-5,980	-8,645	-8,987	-2,807	-245	0	-8,787	-8,890	-8,987
Total	-20,950	-30,580	-31,569	-11,649	-1,704	-678	-32,599	-32,284	-32,247

Released by the Financial Supervisory Service in October 2010

<Table 11> Lawsuits in relation to KIKO

Date	Contents
August 2008	The first lawsuit on KIKO S&T Motors filed a lawsuit against SC Jeil Bank, arguing "We lost 4.8 billion due to an unfair contract."
October 2008	The Court ruled to start a regenerative process for the first time for a company damaged by KIKO Daegu District Court ruled that IDH had to start recovery procedure.
November 2008	97 small and medium-sized companies filed a class action against 13 banks that sold KIKO such as Citi, SC Jeil, Shinhan and Korea Exchange Bank in Seoul Central District Court arguing, "KIKO contracts are invalid."
December 2008	The Court ruled that the banks were responsible for the sale of KIKO for the first time with regard to the injunction filed by Monami and DS LCD against SC Jeil bank.
January 2009	Seoul Central District Court dismissed the injunction to suspend KIKO filed by Jinyang Shipping against Shinhan.
April 2009	Seoul Investment, an investment firm, filed a class action against Jinseong TEC arguing that Jinseong caused losses to investors by falsely announcing quarterly earnings without disclosing losses from KIKO.
April 2009	Court dismissed most of the injunctions against KIKO. Seven cases were dismissed among 10 cases filed by 10 companies against five banks.
February 2010	Seoul Central District Court ruled against the plaintiff, Soosan, for a lawsuit against Woori Bank and Citi Bank for a claim for recapture of wrongful profits.
November 2010	Seoul Central District Court did not acknowledge the unfairness of KIKO in a lawsuit filed by 118 small and medium-sized companies against banks for restitution of unjust enrichment. Court ruled partial responsibilities of banks against 19 companies.
December 2011	Seoul High Court ruled partially for Saeshin Precision in a damage claim suit filed against Shinhan Bank and SC Jeil Bank arguing that KIKO caused 4 billion won in losses.
September 2013	The Supreme Court ruled for banks. KIKO was ruled to be a product suitable for hedging exchange rate risk.
By the end of March 2014	Lawsuits against KIKO include 15 cases in the first trial, eight cases in the second trial and 42 cases in the third trial. 151 companies appealed the case at the first trial and 82 companies appealed the case at the second trial.

(Revised from Kim & Jun, 2012)

3.3 Stock-flow diagrams and simulation of general derivatives

For the simulation of the derivatives, the following <Figure 22> was made. Variables include the general financial conditions of companies. Since the causal loop diagram was made based on financial statements, the Stock-Flow Diagram was constructed considering financial statements, trade receivables and business profit rate. And, changes in exchange rate were added as 'Opposite Change', 'No Change', 'Double Change' to observe the changes according to influences; 'No change' means no changes in exchange rate; 'Opposite Change' means the exchange rate is in a downward direction; 'Double Change' means the exchange rate changes at a doubling speed. Assuming that other conditions are consistent, changes look linear. Foreign account receivables profits are offset with the value of derivatives, which means that non-operating profit does not have an impact. This shows hedge ratio is 1, assuming that it achieved complete hedge. And we can get the results of simulation like <Figure 23>, <Figure 24>, <Figure 25>, and <Figure 26>.

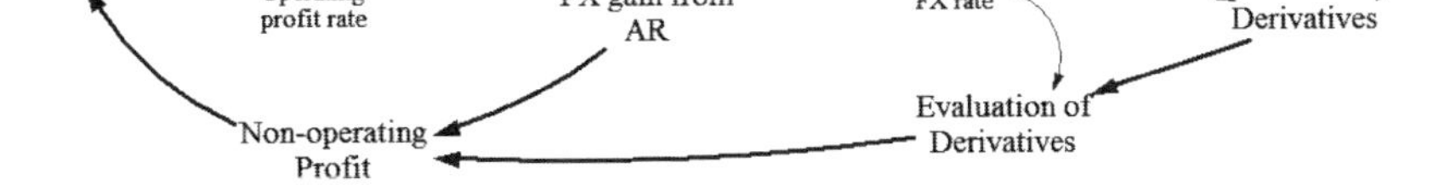

<Figure 22> Stock-flow diagram of general derivatives

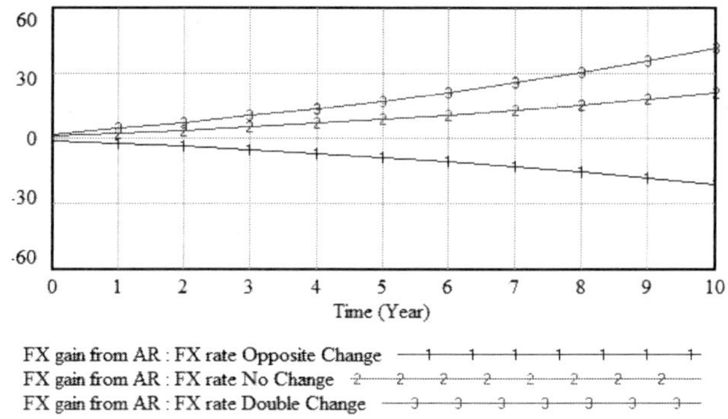

<Figure 23> Simulation results of the profits of foreign exchange AR in accordance with the changes in exchange rate

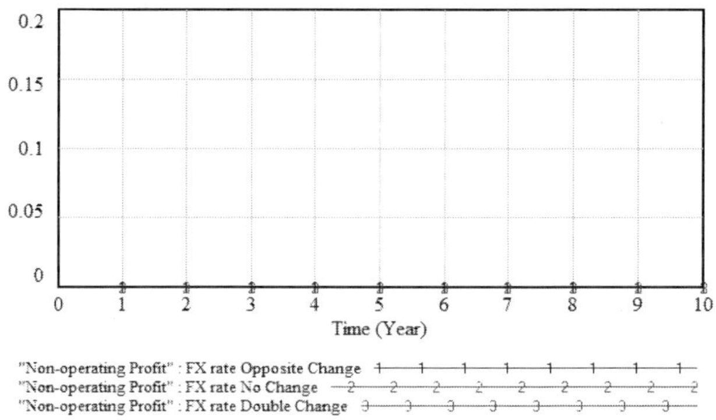

<Figure 24> Simulation results of the evaluation of derivatives in accordance with the changes in exchange rate

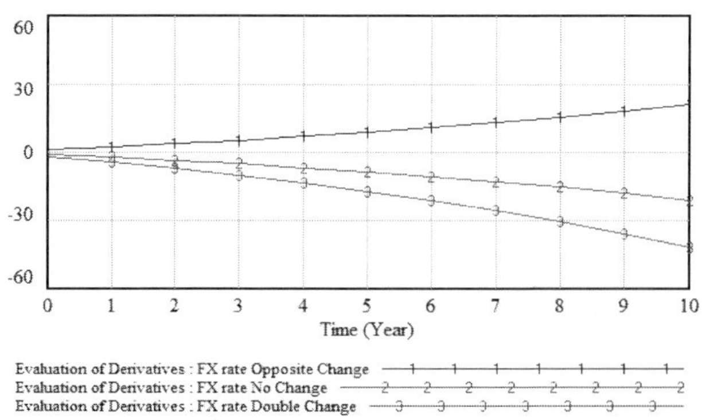

<Figure 25> Simulation results of non-operating profit in accordance with the changes in exchange rate

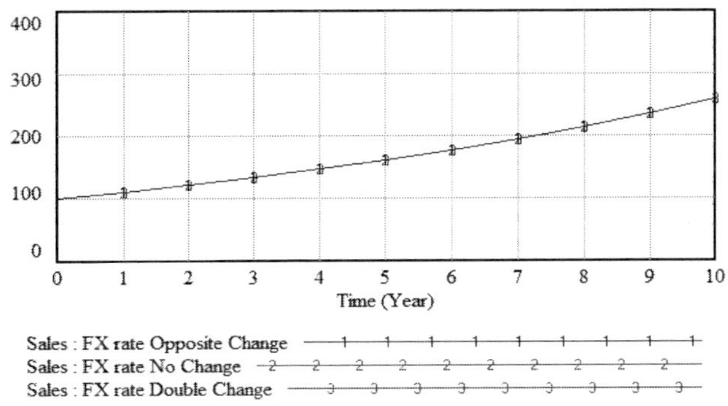

<Figure 26> Simulation results of sales in accordance with the changes in exchange rate

3.4 Stock-flow diagram and simulation of KIKO

Stock-flow diagram <Figure 27> and simulation results of KIKO <Figure 28, 29, 30, 31> are as follows: net income during the term can significantly increase or decrease in accordance with the changes in exchange rate. Accordingly, changes due to exchange rate fluctuation can be huge. If net income during the term are decreased, sales operation can be hampered and, as a result, sales can be reduced. Profits from KIKO lead to excessive purchasing much more than what was planned, which can lead to a significant amount of loss due to a sudden spike in the exchange rate. This could return to the original goal somewhat.

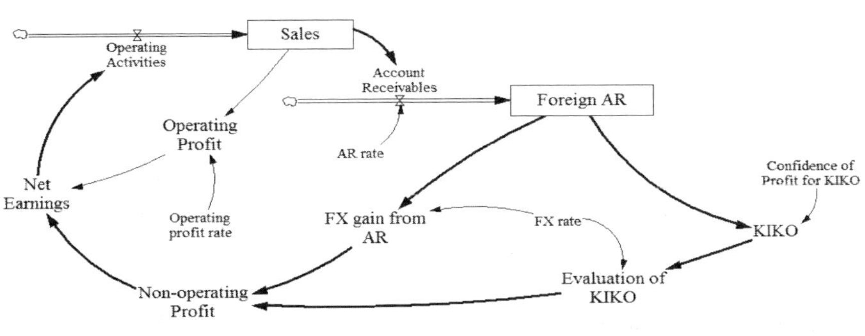

<Figure 27> Stock-flow diagram of KIKO derivatives

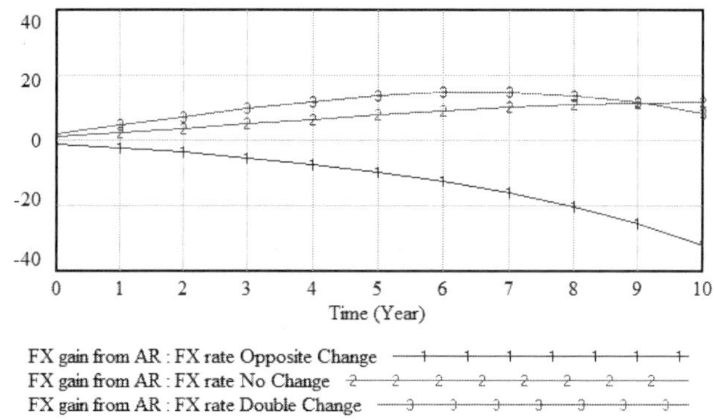

<Figure 28> Simulation results of the profits of foreign currency AR in accordance with the changes in exchange rate

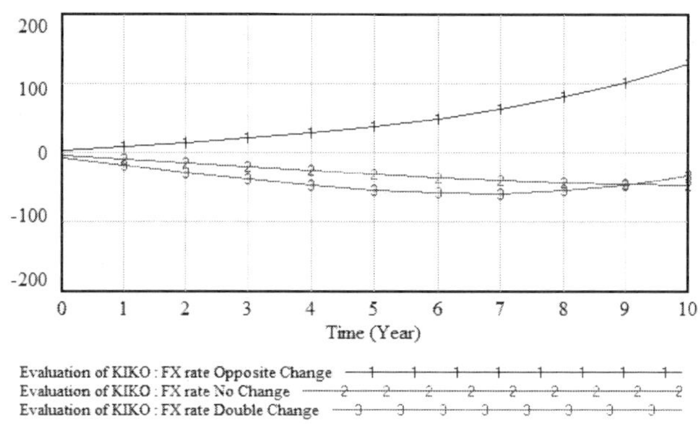

<Figure 29> Simulation results of the evaluation of derivatives in accordance with the changes in exchange rate

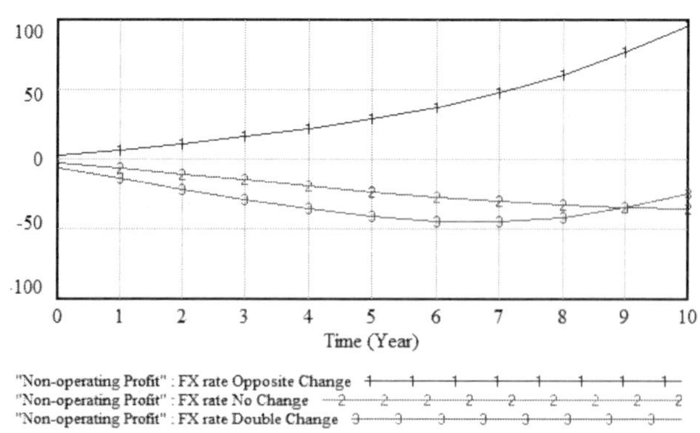

<Figure 30> Simulation results of non-operating profit in accordance with the changes in exchange rate

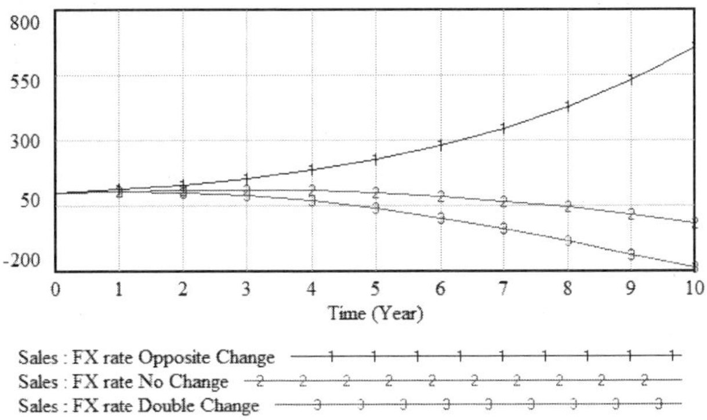

<Figure 31> Simulation results of sales in accordance with the changes in exchange rate

3.5 Simulation scenarios and results

We reviewed the impact of exchange rate on the net income during the term through general derivatives and KIKO. Next is the simulation of the actual exchange rate fluctuation from 2003 to 2012. The results are as follows. <Figure 32> shows the actual exchange rate fluctuation for 10 years, which shows a high increase in the sixth year (2008) and seventh year (2009). At that time, companies considered that the exchange rate could be in a stable condition or in a downward direction. That is why they regarded the product to be favorable in case of a stable or decreasing exchange rate. They did not expect the exchange rate would increase and profits from foreign accounts receivable would decrease risks at a certain level. However, companies make contracts two times as the necessary amount. Even profits from foreign AR could be 110 to 120, the value of KIKO decreases by more than 200. This would result in negative net income during the term. While sales do not change significantly, the risks of KIKO increase to the amount of sales. From <Figure 32> to <Figure 36> shows the results.

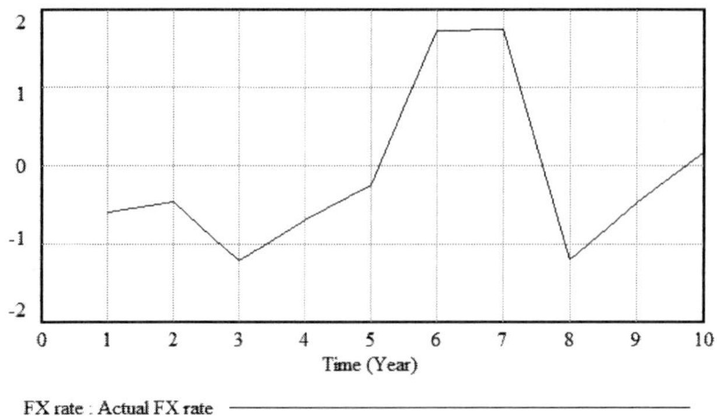

<Figure 32> Exchange rate fluctuations (2003-2012)

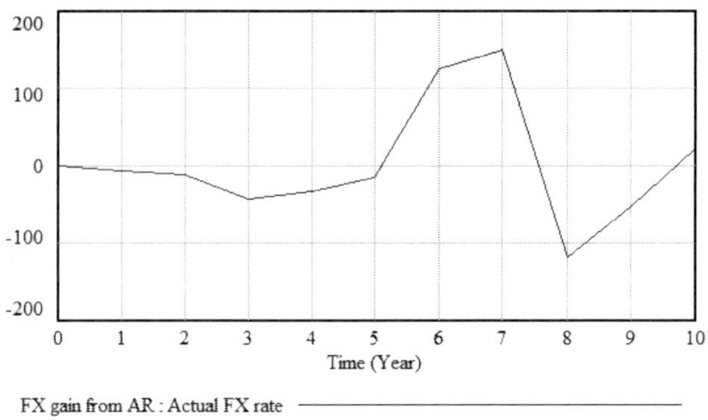

<Figure 33> Simulation results of the profits of foreign currency AR in accordance with the actual changes in exchange rate

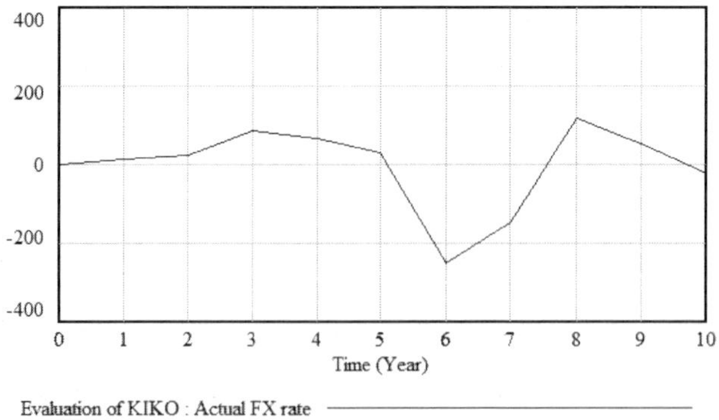

<Figure 34> Simulation results of the evaluation of KIKO in accordance with the actual changes in exchange rate

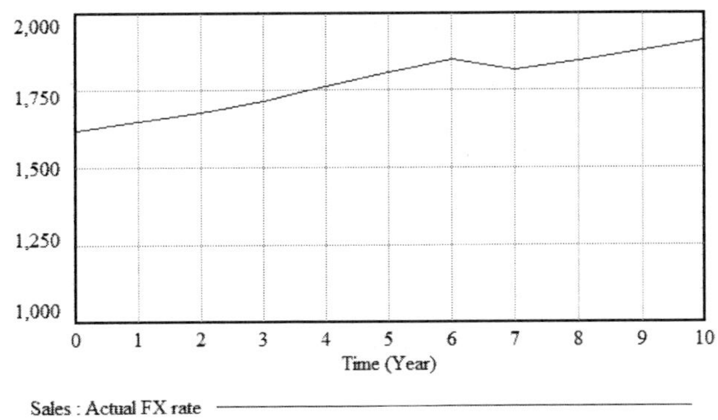

<Figure 35> Simulation results of sales in accordance with the actual changes in exchange rate

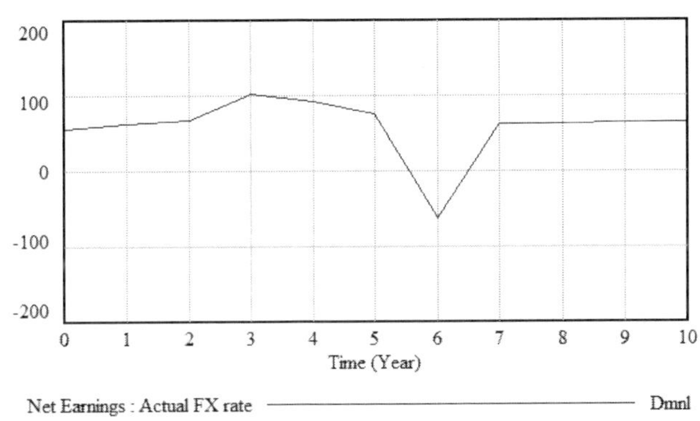

<Figure 36> Simulation results of net income during the term in accordance with the actual changes in exchange rate

3.6 Actual examples of company

<Figure 37> and <Figure 38> show the comparison between the trend line of sales and net income for Monami and the simulations of <Figure 37> and <Figure 38>, which is one of the representative companies that made a KIKO contract. The sales of Monami increased from 162 billion won in 2003 to 205 billion won in 2008. Exports increased as well, which was why it got exposure

increased to foreign exchange. It used KIKO to hedge FX. Until 2006, Monami's net income during the term continued to increase. In 2007, net income started to decrease, and in 2008, it recorded -12.2 billion won including derivatives losses of 6.7 billion won. We can confirm the actual results are similar to the simulated results. This follows the typical structure of limits to growth and reveals a dangerous structure that could generate sharp loss due to KIKO.

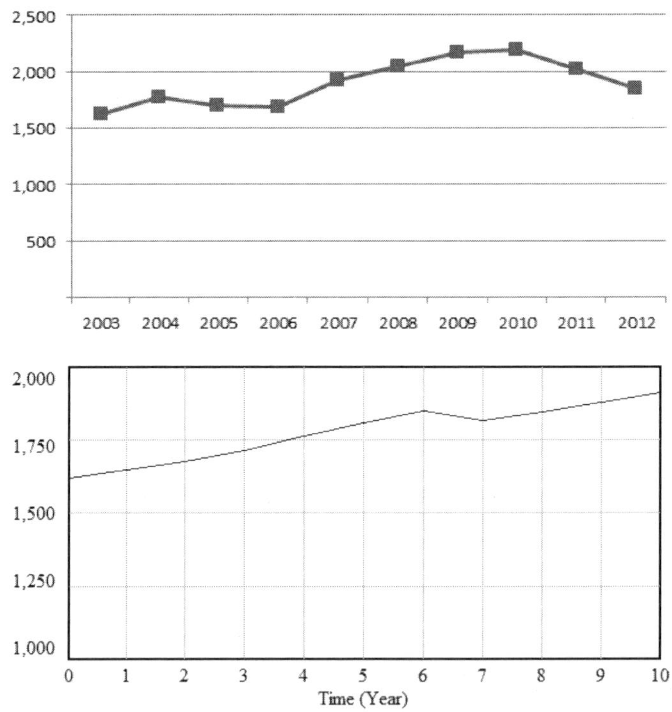

<Figure 37> Trend line of the sales of Monami with Figure 34 (Unit: 100 million won)

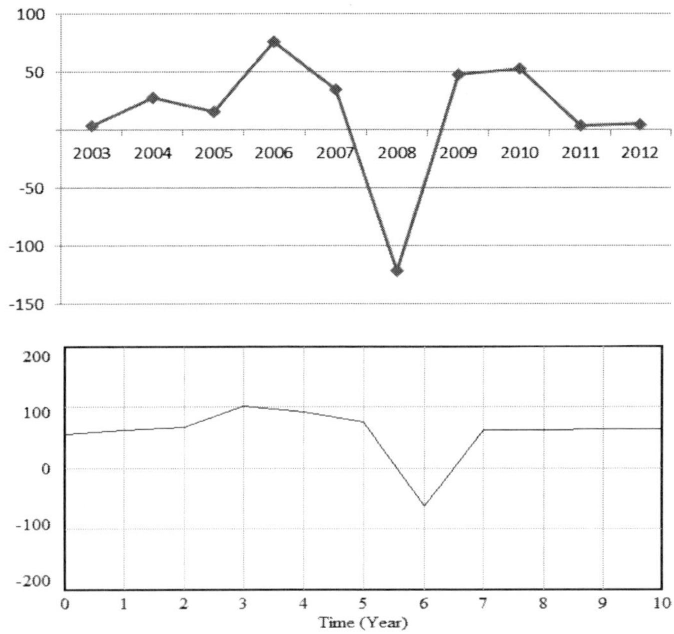

<Figure 38> Trend line of net income of Monami with Figure 35 (Unit: 100 million won)

4. Conclusions and Implications

This study examined the dynamic flows of derivatives. Companies buy derivatives to hedge foreign exchange, which would allow companies to reduce foreign exchange risk. However, if some companies try to make derivatives a means of generating profits with covetous attitudes, rather than a way to avoid risks, the risk can become huge. However, banks do not say the high risk for getting their profit, sometimes. Financial specialists of companies should understand this.

Through simulation methods suggested in this study, companies can understand the impact of derivatives in accordance with the changes of exchange rate.

Since the simulation method is not difficult, it will be easy to predict risks.

The Limits to Growth archetype of system dynamics articulates a structure where there could be accumulated risk during growth. Companies using KIKO show similar types. While companies kept focusing on growth or profit, the danger of KIKO was accumulated; when it reached the threshold, losses became significant, even great enough to cause the bankruptcy of a company. Leverage effects that derivatives have sometimes deliver profits to companies. But, they can cause a great amount of loss unintentionally. Therefore, it is imperative to understand financial structures of companies, comprehend the structure of FX risk management through systems thinking, expect behavior over time in a systematic structure, and make efforts to establish appropriate measures when detecting signals. We need to consider that the exchange rate can suddenly fluctuate. Companies need to be ready for sudden changes in exchange rate.

Sales activities of companies are important. We need to know that endless observation on B loop is necessary for continual sales activity. In addition, financial institutions should give companies the information of evaluating the risks of derivatives. If they understood the structure, threshold, and R loop and B loop through system dynamics, they would have known the inherent risks of KIKO fully. This study has implications that the understanding of KIKO structure would help to understand other derivatives in the future.

V Empirical Study

1. Introduction

The financial crisis that began in the United States in 2008 gave a lot of impacts on the world economy. In Korea, by this impact, radical fluctuations in the exchange rate took place, and many companies had experienced foreign exchange gains or loss. And, the financial state of the company became unstable. In Korea with high weight of exports and imports, the impact by fluctuations in exchange rates is very huge. When looking from <Table 12>, in Korea, compared to nominal GDP, the trade dependence on which was 51.7% in 2002 reached to 85.6% in 2008. After the financial crisis, the trade dependence fell for a while, and it was closer to 81.5% in 2010. Thus, depending on the currency fluctuation, companies can experience many losses.

When the foreign exchange crisis had come in 1997, it also leaded many companies to bankruptcy (Kim, Y., 2003). To examine the effect of exchange rate-related corporate finance in such Korea situation has important meaning.

So far, many papers have studied the exchange exposure of companies. However, in the conventional exchange exposure studies, since it is measured on the basis of the price-earnings ratio of the company, there is a limit in directly looking at the impact on the financial statements of the company. Factors

<Table 12> Foreign Trade Ratio of Nominal GDP for Korea

Year	Nominal GDP ($ Million)	Export		Import		Foreign trade dependency (%)
		Amount ($ Million)	Ratio (%)	Amount ($ Million)	Ratio (%)	
2010	1,094,300	466,384	42.6	425,212	38.9	81.5
2009	902,300	363,534	40.3	323,085	35.8	76.1
2008	1,001,700	422,007	42.1	435,275	43.5	85.6
2007	1,122,700	371,489	33.1	356,846	31.8	64.9
2006	1,011,000	325,465	32.2	309,383	30.6	62.8
2005	898,000	284,419	31.7	261,238	29.1	60.8
2004	765,300	253,845	33.2	224,463	29.3	62.5
2003	680,400	193,817	28.5	178,827	26.3	54.8
2002	608,900	162,471	26.7	152,126	25.0	51.7

Source : Koran Trade Association

influencing on the price-earnings ratio are very diverse. Depending on the cases, the effect of positive (+) or effect of negative (-) are relatively appeared. In the existing studies, that there is a limit to get the significant value of the exchange exposure is because of these reasons. Here, for the exchange rate of the company, this book studies how the exchange rate fluctuation directly impacts on the financial statements of the company. This is because the performance of company shows through the financial statements of the company.

In addition, the net income of company is related to the price-earnings ratio (Paek, Lee, & Park, 2001). And, in most companies, there are foreign exchange gains or losses, which shows that fluctuations in the exchange rate has had a direct effect on the income statement of company (Jeong, Bae, & Lim, 2012).

Here, this study tries to examine the foreign currency assets and foreign currency debt that affect the financial statements of companies, and the foreign exchange gains and losses through derivatives and the correlation. Through these, it is because it looks at how the effect of derivatives before and after the financial crisis shows actual impact on the company. And, it tries to examine the adjustment effect of exchange rate fluctuations in the influence of the foreign currency assets and foreign exchange gains and losses. This, together with the exchange exposure that has been many handled in the previous studies, is to explore the impact of exchange rate fluctuation by the foreign currency asset ratio.

Thus, in this study which includes listed company in Stock Exchange and companies registered in KOSDAQ, with the target of the companies in non-financial manufacturing industry, it is actually to analyze the influences between the relevant factors in the financial statements, through the exchange rate fluctuation from companies. It can provide different viewpoints from previous studies have been made of the exchange exposure.

It can give an implication for companies to prepare for such financial crisis. Since the data used in this study is the data connected in time horizon for the cross-section data, the heteroscedasticity problem that can appear in the cross-section data, and the serial correlation problem of time-series data can occur at the same time. Therefore, this study will use the method of analyzing in forming the balanced panel data that combines the time-series and cross-section data. For the panel data used in this study, it is a balance panel data. The data has been structured the cross section unit of 443 companies in non-financial sectors that are listed in Korea Stock Exchange Market or registered in KOSDAQ market, from 2003 to the end of 2010, which of each company has a time series of eight years. For a statistical package for panel data analysis, it used STATA12.0. The data required for the analysis used each company's financial statements that have extracted from FNGUIDE.

This book is constructed as follows. In 2. design of empirical study, it introduces a method of designing a study associated with the panel analysis, and in 3. empirical analysis results, it analyzes the empirical results. in 4. implication and limitation of study, it will discuss the conclusions and limitation of the study.

2. Design of Empirical Study

2.1 Selection of sample companies and analysis target period

This study selected 443 companies of non-financial industries which are listed in Korea Stock Exchange Market or registered in KOSDAQ market, from 2003 to the end of 2010.

1) As of the end of 2010, companies of non-financial industries which are listed in Korea Stock Exchange Market or registered in KOSDAQ market
2) Corporations that we can acquire the accounting data because they have continually published closing materials since 2003.
3) Corporations that have 8 years of export in their financial reports. It is because there are foreign accounts receivables on export. This chapter explains the relationship between foreign accounts receivables and foreign exchange gain.

The reason why excluded the companies in the bank, insurance, and securities industries, is because the foreign currency assets in the bank, insurance, and securities industries can be handled as normal products, and thus its characteristics can be different from that of the foreign currency assets that are resulted from business activities.

In this study, the analysis period is 8 years between 2003 and 2010, and it used the balanced panel data that each company has a time series of 8 years, by structuring 443 individual companies in the cross-section unit. The reason why the data between 2003 and 2010 is be used because the exchange rate in 2003 to 2006 was relatively stable, and during the period of 2007 to 2010, we can have a look a clear influence relationship before and after the Financial Crisis caused by Lehman Brothers in 2008. It also seems to be meaningful to try to analyze these two periods as its target.

2.2 Setting of hypothesis

The relationship between the foreign exchange gains and corporate financial statements can be seen to as different in the effect depending on the types of items. Also, it could be different due to the causes that occur. Foreign currency assets, in general, are generated through the sales activities of the company. However, foreign currency liabilities are often foreign currency borrowing rather than coming from the purchase activity of company. <Table 13> shows the trend of the entire period of foreign currency accounts receivable amount. From 2003 until 2010, the amount of foreign currency accounts receivable of target companies grew by 352%. This can be understood that the foreign currency accounts receivable amount is getting bigger, as the weight of exports expands. <Table 13> shows that the foreign currency receivables were surging up in between 2005 and 2006, and between 2008 and 2009. Because the export ratio was stabilized in stable exchange rates. In 2008 and 2009, there seems to be an increase in the exchange rate which affected exports. <Table 12> shows the export to GDP ratio increased from 20% to 30% in 2004, and to 40% in 2008.

In addition, the export amount had been also increased significantly.

<Table 13> Trend of the amount of foreign currency accounts receivable for the entire period

Unit: 1 Billion won

Year	2003	2004	2005	2006	2007	2008	2009	2010
Foreign asset amount	6,557	6,891	9,481	12,357	13,628	18,393	24,469	23,087
Growth rate		5%	38%	30%	10%	35%	33%	-6%

Foreign currency accounts receivables are the balance amount as of the end of the fiscal year. It can also be understood as the financial items occurring through business activities of the company. Companies often collect in foreign currency for trade receivables while exporting goods. And foreign exchange gains also have relationship with derivatives profits. Companies buy derivatives by determining the extent of foreign currency assets. If derivatives are purchased, it also affects the derivatives profits to the foreign exchange gains. In the future, the more companies' exports, the more the foreign currency accounts receivable will increase. The foreign currency assets' impact on the foreign exchange gains is also believed to increase. It can expect the explanatory power by the below hypotheses.

In the existing studies, the studies on the foreign currency liabilities were many (Kwon, 2006a; Yu & Hong, 2009). However, the foreign currency assets of companies will affect the foreign exchange gains of companies (Song & Cho, 2011). This is because companies would have foreign currency assets due to the occurrence of trade receivables in foreign currency with such as exports, and through this, in the companies, the foreign exchange gains would occur naturally. In particular, to Korean companies that have higher export dependency than export dependency, it can be considered that the foreign currency assets had a bigger impact on the foreign exchange gains than the foreign currency liabilities did. As confirmed by <Table 13>, the hypothesis can be made that the foreign currency assets have had a significant impact on the foreign exchange gains as it increased rapidly.

[Hypothesis 1] The proportion of foreign currency assets during the period affected the foreign exchange gain ratio.

Lee & Park (2009) studied the effects that the exchange rate fluctuation gave to the exchange exposure determinants. The foreign currency assets that companies have will have a direct impact whenever the exchange rate fluctuation occurs. Accordingly, this research tries to check the adjustment effect of foreign currency assets ratio between the exchange rate fluctuation rate and the foreign exchange gains ratio for the impact of such exchange rates. Through this, we can weigh up the impact that the foreign currency assets ratio can give on the foreign exchange gain ratio, depending on the exchange rate fluctuation. Only with the fact that companies simply have foreign currency assets, the foreign exchange gains and losses do not occur. The foreign currency gains and losses are to be determined in accordance with the rise or fall of the exchange rate.

[Hypothesis 2] The foreign currency assets ratio would be moderated by the exchange rate fluctuation ratio in affecting the foreign exchange gain ratio during that period.

2.3 Analysis model

2.3.1 Setting of analysis model

In order to verify the hypotheses presented above, this research sets the following model. [Model 1], by using the panel data, in a situation in which controls the export ratio, foreign currency liabilities ratio, and derivatives profit ratio, is a model for the analysis of the foreign currency assets ratio and the foreign exchange gains ratio. In this case, t-phase error term of i company, to be able to reflect individual specific effect over the time, and the time specific effect for each company in a complex manner, was included in the model by dividing into the company effect(ηi), time effect(λt), and the error(ϱt).

[Model 1]

$$FXGit = \alpha+\beta 1FARit+\beta 2EXPit+\beta 3FLRit+\beta 4DERit+\beta 5FXRit+\eta i+\lambda t+\varrho it$$

FXGit : FX gain ratio in t-phase of i company (=foreign exchange gain /revenue)
FARit : Foreign currency dominated asset ratio in t-phase of i company (=foreign currency assets /total assets)
EXPit : Export ratio in t-phase of i company (=export amount /revenue)
FLRit : Foreign currency dominated liability ratio in t-phase of i company (=foreign currency liabilities amount /total assets)
DERit : Derivatives profit ratio in t-phase of i company (=derivatives profit /total assets)
FXRit : FX rate fluctuation rate in t-phase of i company (USD/KRW fluctuation rate compared to previous year)
ηi : Individual specific effect of i company
λt : Time specific effect of t-phase
ϱt : Remaining error

2.3.2 Suitability verification method of the analysis model

The panel data analysis methods arc diverse whether the constant items are same as cross section or time-series, and the assumption about the structure of the error item. The first step to estimate the suitability of the model is to verify whether the individual specific effect(ηi) and the time specific effect (λt) exist within the model. In other words, when setting the null hypothesis (H0)$\sigma\eta 2=\sigma\lambda^2$

=0, and adopting the null hypothesis, since there is no individual specific effect and time specific effect, it is possible to obtain efficient estimates in the general least squares method (OLS). However, when the null hypothesis is rejected, the error term becoming to like ηi+λt+ϱit, and because of the presence of ηi and λt, it cannot obtain efficient estimates in the general least squares method (OLS). Test on these hypotheses can be made by Lagrange Multiplier Test that Breusch & Pagan (1980) presented, and the statistics, g, of the formula (1) shows asymptotically $\chi^2(2)$ distribution.

When using the statistics g of formula (1) in separating by two terms, it can also test the null hypothesis of $\sigma^2\eta=^2$ and $\sigma^2\lambda\eta$ $\chi^2(1)$, respectively. If the presence of ηi and λt in the model can be identified, in the second step, it has to test to estimate ηi and λt by the fixed effect model or dummy variable model, or to do random effect model or variance components model. Fixed effect model is a model to use the least squares dummy variable (LSDV) as the parameter estimate method, by assuming that ηi and λt are fixed. Probability effect model, assuming ηi and λt as the probability variables, is a model that utilizes the generalized lease squares (GLS) as the parameter estimate method.

$$g=\frac{NT}{2(N-1)}\left[\frac{\sum_{i=1}^{N}\left(\sum_{t=1}^{T}\mu_{it}\right)^2}{\sum_{i=1}^{N}\sum_{t=1}^{T}\mu_{it}^2}-1\right]^2+\frac{NT}{2(N-1)}\left[\frac{\sum_{t=1}^{N}\left(\sum_{i=1}^{T}\mu_{it}\right)^2}{\sum_{t=1}^{N}\sum_{i=1}^{T}\mu_{it}^2}-1\right]^2\sim\chi^2(2) \qquad (1)$$

N: number of companies, T: number of the years, µit: least squared residuals

In order to compare the suitability of two models, by setting the null hypothesis (H0: $E(\eta i/\lambda t)=0$) that there is no correlation between the individual specific variable(ηi) and time specific variable (λt), it is to carry out Hausman Test. If the null hypothesis that $E(\eta i/\lambda t)=0$ is adopted, it is desirable to estimate by the probability effect model because GLS estimates become to have the consistency and efficiency by the probability effect model. If the null hypothesis is rejected, since GLS estimates become to have the inconsistency, the estimation by the fixed effect model becomes desirable (Hausman, 1978).

In order to check the suitability of the fixed effect model, by setting the null hypothesis (H0): $\eta 1 = \eta 2 = *** = \eta N-1 = 0$ and $\lambda 1=\lambda 2=***=\lambda T=0$, it can perform F- test. In this case, if the null hypothesis is rejected, it can be interpreted that the fixed effect exists.

2.4 Analysis target variables

2.4.1 Foreign Exchange Gain

For the impact on the foreign exchange gains of company by the fluctuations in foreign exchange rates, it used the foreign exchange gain ratio (FXG). The foreign exchange gain ratio was measured by dividing the foreign exchange gains of company by the total sales of company. Foreign exchange gains correspond to a non-operating profit in the financial statements of company, and it directly affects on the corporate profits. The foreign exchange gains might affect the corporate value as the result. In the existing exchange exposure studies (Kwon, 1998), they utilized the price-earnings ratio of company as the dependent variable. Here, since it is a study on the exchange rate fluctuation impact on the financial statements of company, it is supposed to measure the foreign exchange gains rather than price-earnings ratio.

2.4.2 Foreign Currency Asset

The foreign currency-denominated bonds are increased in accordance with the export of company. Foreign currency-denominated bonds, which account for most of the foreign currency assets, depending on the fluctuations in the exchange rate, increase or decrease the foreign exchange gains. The foreign currency assets can be an important factor in the exchange exposure determinants. Through this study, I tries to confirm this. Song & Cho (2011) have revealed that foreign currency assets were significant factors, depending on the times. Here, this study attempted to examine in the foreign currency assets ratio. This is because the influence of the scale, rather than the influence of amount in each company, can give impact on the foreign exchange gain ratio. Foreign currency assets ratio was measured by dividing the foreign currency assets by the total assets of the company.

2.4.3 Control variables

The variables that give changes to the foreign currency gains, not only currency assets, but some other variables can exist. As the control variables, it used the export ratio, derivatives profit ratio, foreign currency liabilities ratio, and exchange rate fluctuation rate. These are items that have been mentioned as determinants of exchange exposure in existing studies (Kwon, 1998).

(1) Export ratio

Depending on the export ratio of companies, the foreign exchange gain ratio of companies can be affected. When the export weight of company increases, the foreign currency accounts receivables are generated. This is what can give an indirect effect on the exchange exposure (Lee, 2003). As shown in <Table 12>, Korea's trade dependence is high, and it has higher degree of dependence in exports than imports. In other words, rather than the impact of foreign currency fluctuations coming from imports, the effects coming from exports can be guessed to be bigger.

(2) Foreign currency liabilities ratio

Foreign currency liabilities are a factor that gives a lot of influence on the exchange exposure like the foreign currency assets. Kwon (2007) studied on the asymmetry of exchange rate and the foreign currency-denominated liabilities, and Kwon (2013) studied the influence that the use of foreign currency liabilities gives on the corporate value. Depending on the degree of foreign currency liabilities, the impact on the foreign exchange gains can be very big.

(3) Derivatives profit ratio

Companies, if the risk of exchange exposure is increased, register derivatives as a financial strategy in order to avoid the risk. This is intended to have a role as a hedge by increasing the derivatives too when the foreign currency assets increase. If the foreign currency assets have a positive (+) effect on the exchange exposure, the derivatives profit ratio can give the negative effect on the exchange exposure (Roh, Yun & Kim, 1998).

(4) Exchange rate fluctuation ratio

Fluctuations in foreign currency give a direct impact on the foreign exchange gains of company. If owning foreign currency assets, when the exchange rate increases, the company will have the foreign exchange gains. Looking in <Table 14>, it is possible to check the fluctuations in the currency during the entire period.

<Table 14> Fluctuation rate for three currencies in the entire sample period (2003-2010)

Year	USD	YEN	EUR
2003	-1.2%	11.2%	17.8%
2004	-12.4%	-8.7%	-3.7%
2005	-2.5%	-15.7%	-14.6%
2006	-9.9%	-8.7%	0.9%
2007	0.5%	5.2%	10.4%
2008	41.0%	64.1%	32.0%
2009	-15.5%	-13.7%	-7.5%
2010	-1.3%	6.3%	-11.3%

For the exchange rate used here, it showed the annual average exchange rates of the currency that the Bank of Korea notified. Although the exchange rate fluctuations are frequently performed, it is possible to check that USD, YEN, and EUR have caused a big change in 2008. USD, YEN, EUR are sometimes also seen as that have appeared different in their fluctuation direction. Although USD was relatively stable period with -0.2% in 2003, YEN and EUR increased to 10.5% and 19.5%, respectively. In addition, although, in 2006, EUR was relatively stable time with 1.9%, USD and YEN decreased to -8.2% and -9.1%. The foreign currency assets that companies have are very diverse, but here, I used thc fluctuation rate in the exchange rate for USD, as a statistical variable. This is because most of the companies use USD as the settlement currency.

This study divided and compared the entire period (2003 to 2010) into two periods, sub-period from 2003 to 2006 and from 2006 and 2010. Being divided into two periods into account come from the financial crisis in 2008. Since 2003 the exchange rate was relatively stable downward trend. Korean economics which finished the IMF early had been increasing, and various economic indicators were stable. Since 2007, the signs of the financial crisis was occurred. The global economy was starting to get nervous. Stabilized exchange rates were being started up to increase around 2007. Finally, global economy fell in darkness from the bankruptcy of Lehman Brothers in 2008. So, this study sets up two sub-periods from 2003 to 2010. It makes sense to look into both periods from 2003 to 2006 as the first sub-period and from 2007 to 2010 as a sub-period 2. It has the meaningful comparison.

3. Empirical analysis results

3.1 Descriptive statistics of each variable

When summarizing the descriptive statistics for each variable for the total samples, in this study, are as <Table 15>.

In <Table 15>, The mean of the foreign exchange gain ratio (FXG) in the entire period was -0.04%. It was + 0.04% in the sub-period 1, but -0.11% in the sub-period 2. This is because the contrast effects appeared in the sub-period 1 and 2. Although it seemed that there is no major difference to the entire between the sub-period 1 and 2, in the sub-period 2, the foreign exchange gain ratio appears in a minus.

The foreign currency assets ratio (FAR), during the entire period, is almost 0% in minimum to 100% in maximum, and the mean showed as 6.49%.

<Table 15> Descriptive statistics of each variable

Variable	Period	Obs	Mean	Std. Dev.	Min	Max
FXG	Entire period	3544	-0.0004	0.0284	-0.5990	0.4674
	Sub-Period 1	1772	0.0004	0.0214	-0.3760	0.4674
	Sub-Period 2	1772	-0.0011	0.0340	-0.5990	0.3778
FAR	Entire period	3544	0.0649	0.0813	0.0000	0.9170
	Sub-Period 1	1772	0.0630	0.0822	0.0000	0.9170
	Sub-Period 2	1772	0.0667	0.0805	0.0000	0.6870
EXP	Entire period	3544	0.3910	0.2955	0.0000	1.0000
	Sub-Period 1	1772	0.3794	0.2941	0.0000	1.0000
	Sub-Period 2	1772	0.4026	0.2965	0.0003	1.0000
FLR	Entire period	3544	0.0712	0.0892	0.0000	0.9061
	Sub-Period 1	1772	0.0689	0.0848	0.0000	0.8645
	Sub-Period 2	1772	0.0735	0.0934	0.0000	0.9061
DER	Entire period	3544	-0.0061	0.0451	-0.7170	0.2751
	Sub-Period 1	1772	0.0019	0.0097	-0.0677	0.0921
	Sub-Period 2	1772	-0.0111	0.0564	-0.7170	0.2751
FXR	Entire period	3544	-0.0014	0.1653	-0.1547	0.4104
	Sub-Period 1	1772	-0.0650	0.0479	-0.1243	-0.0117
	Sub-Period 2	1772	0.0621	0.2105	-0.1547	0.4104

Note. The data, by targeting the non-financial industries' companies out of the listed companies and registered company in FNGUIDE, was extracted the related contents in the financial statements between 2003 and 2010.

Export ratio (EXP) shows approximately 39% as the average. It was slightly decreased into 37.94% in the sub-period 1, but it was slightly increased to 40.26% in the sub-period 2. <Table 12> explains the rate in the sub-period 2 is higher than sub-period 1. It is assumed that the export rates of the companies were increased.

Foreign currency liabilities ratio (FLR) was about 7.12% in the entire period. Considering that the FAR was 6.49%, FLR was somewhat high. I could guess what the proportion of the import was as high as the proportion of the export. Because there was no data for the turnover rate of the foreign currency assets and foreign currency liability, it is difficult to guess how big the trading scales were.

Derivatives profit ratio (DER) was 0.61% in the entire period. However, it was 0.19%. And it was increased to −1.11% in the sub-period 2 significantly.

This was that companies purchased derivatives for the risk management. It is assumed that DER was the bigger impact from the fluctuation of exchange rate during the financial crisis period particularly.

The mean of the Exchange rate fluctuation rate (FXR) was −0.14% in the entire period, −6.5% in the sub-period 1, and +6.2% in the sub-period 2. Looking for FXR, the standard deviation was 4.8%, but 21% in the sub-period 2. It can be assumed that the exchange rate fluctuations was great in the sub-period 2. <Table 14> explained the fact.

The correlation between variables that were calculated using the data of the entire sample periods (2003 to 2010) of each variable included in this study is as <Table 16>.

During the entire period, the weight of exports (EXP) is significant as 52.63% to the foreign currency assets ratio (FAR), and the derivatives profit ratio (DER) was significant with the foreign exchange gain ratio (FXG), foreign currency assets ratio (FAR), and the weight of exports (EXP). Foreign exchange rate fluctuation ratio (FXR) appeared as significant with the foreign exchange gain ratio (FXG) and derivatives profit rate (DER). In the sub-period 1, it appeared that the foreign currency assets ratio (FAR) is significant with the foreign exchange gain ratio (FXG), and the foreign currency liabilities ratio (FLR) is appeared to be significant with the weight of exports (EXP), which is guessed that the exports are connected to the purchase in the foreign currency. The derivatives profit ratio (DER) and foreign currency liabilities ratio (FLR) were significant in the sub-period 1 and the sub-period 2.

<Table 16> Correlation coefficient between variables during the period

Entire period (2003-2010)

	FXG	FAR	EXP	FLR	DER	FXR
FXG	1					
FAR	-0.0337*	1				
EXP	-0.0002	0.5263***	1			
FLR	0.0024	0.2710***	0.1511***	1		
DER	-0.1904***	-0.0765***	-0.0921***	0.0337	1	
FXR	-0.0167	0.0177	0.0168	0.0331*	-0.3116***	1

Note. These are tables of the correlation coefficient between the variables which were calculated for the entire sample period between 2003 and 2010.

*Significant at p <.01. **Signigicant at p <.05. ***Significant p <.001.

Sub-period 1 (2003-2006)

	FXG	FAR	EXP	FLR	DER	FXR
FXG	1					
FAR	-0.2361***	1				
EXP	-0.0884***	-0.5268***	1			
FLR	0.1607***	0.2854***	0.1689***	1		
DER	0.1957***	0.1525***	0.2089***	0.0045	1	
FXR	-0.0074	0.0124	-0.0133	0.0045	-0.1272***	1

Note. These are tables of the correlation coefficient between the variables which were calculated for the entire sample period between 2003 and 2006.

*Significant at p <.01. **Signigicant at p <.05. ***Significant p <.001.

Sub-period 2 (2007-2010)

	FXG	FAR	EXP	FLR	DER	FXR
FXG	1					
FAR	0.1101***	1				
EXP	0.0566**	0.5251***	1			
FLR	-0.1012***	0.2572***	0.1334***	1		
DER	-0.2531***	-0.1198***	-0.1576***	0.0426	1	
FXR	-0.0073	0.0116	0.0056	0.0337	-0.2856***	1

Note. These are tables of the correlation coefficient between the variables which were calculated for the entire sample period between 2007 and 2010.

*Significant at p <.01. **Signigicant at p <.05. ***Significant p <.001.

3.2 Suitability test results of the model

<Table 17> is a result of testing the suitability of the model for the entire period (2003 to 2010). Also, it tried to examine the suitability of the model even in the sub-period 1 and sub-period 2 together.

<Table 17> Suitability test results of the model for the period
[Model 2]
$FXGit = \alpha + \beta 1FARit + \beta 2EXPit + \beta 3FLRit + \beta 4DERit + \beta 5FXRit + \eta i + \lambda t + \varrho it$

Category	Lagrange multiplier Test (H0 : σ^2=0)	Hausman Test (H0 : E(ηi/χit)=0)	F-Test (H0 : ηi=0)
	g statistics	m statistics	F value
Entire period	5.59***	9.92*	1.43***
Sub-period 1	7.56***	15.04**	2.12***
Sub-period 2	0.00	13.96**	0.68

Note. *Significant at p <.01. **Signigicant at p <.05. ***Significant p <.001.

Looking at the lagrange multiplier test results for the entire period in the first column, it shows the result that g statistics rejects the null hypothesis. This means that $\eta\eta i$ exists in all of the two periods, which can know that there is a need to test the suitability of the fixed effects model and the probability effects model by Hausman Test. In addition, the sub-period 1 in a significance level of 1%, and the sub-period 2 in a significance level of 10%, can reject the null hypothesis.

The second column, under the null hypothesis that $E(\eta\eta i/\chi\chi it)=0$, is a result of performing Housman Test for each model. Looking at the Housman Test results for the entire periods, m value of the model is 9.92, which shows the result that the null hypothesis is rejected at the significance level of 10%. Therefore, since it can be said that it has a significant correlation between the individual specific effects and independent variables, it is possible to know that the coefficient estimation by the fixed effects model. It was confirmed that the sub-period 1 and sub-period 2 were also significant.

Looking at the third column, that is, the result that performed the F-test by setting the null hypothesis $\eta\eta$i = 0 in order to confirm the suitability of the fixed effects model, the F values of each model showed the results that rejected the null hypothesis. The F value is 1.43 in the entire period, and with 2.12 in the sub-period 1. However, 0.68 in the sub-period 2, respectively, rejects the null hypothesis.

So far, in the entire period (2003 to 2010) and the sub-period 1 (2003 to 2006), it performed Lagrange Test, Housman Test, and F-test, since it confirmed that the coefficient estimation by the fixed effects model is all suitable, and the sub-period 2 (2007 to 2010) is only through hausman. If it is considered the financial crisis during the period. There is no problem in analyzing by the fixed effects model.

3.3 Results of the empirical analysis of fixed effects model

<Table 18> is the results that analyzed the relationship between the foreign currency assets and foreign currency gain by the fixed effects model for the target of the entire period (2003 to 2010). The regression coefficient of the foreign exchange gain ratio (FXG) that was measured by the foreign exchange assets ratio (FAR) is found to be significant at 5% significance level with 3.58%(t=2.51). In the case of the control variables, as the variables that significantly affect the foreign exchange gains, the weight of exports (EXP) and

derivatives profit ratio (DER) appeared to be significant. This is because companies, in general, by registering derivatives for foreign currency assets or foreign currency liabilities, are in a trend of hedge for the foreign exchange gain. In relation to the negative, the regression coefficient of the foreign exchange gain ratio (FXG) that was measured by derivatives profit rate, was appeared to be significant at the 1% significance level, with -0.1232(t = -7.85).

<Table 18> The result of panel analysis between the foreign currency asset ratio and the foreign exchange profits ratio using the fixed effects model

Category	Entire period	Sub-period 1	Sub-period 2
Constant	.0009(0.22)	.0110(-0.91*)	.0076(1.01)
FAR	.0358(2.51**)	-.0114(-0.55)	.0558(2.13**)
EXP	-.0112(-1.50)	-.0235(-2.25**)	-.0269(-1.82*)
FLR	.0171(1.32)	.0371(1.66*)	.0023(0.10)
DER	-.1232(-7.85***)	.5998(0.53)	-.1348(-7.09***)
FXR	-.0135(-3.46**)	.0098(0.53)	-.0164(-3.48***)
F value	14.39***	7.08***	11.53***
R^2	.0341	.0894	.0549

Note. *Significant at p <.01. **Signigicant at p <.05. ***Significant p <.001.

In <Table 18>, As a result of panel analysis for the entire period between the foreign currency assets ratio and foreign exchange gain ratio using the fixed effects model, it has a relationship (+). Through this, it can be guessed that the exchange rate fluctuation gave a bigger impact on which period. If looking in the sub-period 1, as the exchange rate fluctuation rate (FXR) has a positive relationship, FAR also becomes a negative relationship, and if looking in the sub-period 2, although the foreign currency asset ratio (FAR) has a negative relationship, as the exchange fluctuation rate in the sub-period 2 gives bigger impact on the exchange rate fluctuation rate (FXR), it shows a negative(-)relationship in the entire period. This, as seen in <Table 14>, in the sub-period 1, the exchange rate fluctuation appears mainly in Negative, and in the sub-period 2, it appears in Positive, which is seemed that the foreign exchange gain ratio (FXG) was affected by the exchange rate fluctuation rate (FXR). Here, it can be guessed that the exchange rate fluctuation rate (FXR) has the moderating effect between the foreign currency assets ratio(FAR) and foreign exchange gain ratio(FXG).

<Table 19> is the result of having performed the stepwise panel analysis in order to reconfirm the relationship between the foreign exchange gains and each variable that have been shown from the results of the entire period panel analysis by the fixed effects model. In the stepwise, this research tries to verify the interaction effect (FAR * FXR) of the foreign currency assets ratio and exchange rate fluctuation rate, together. As the verification result, the interaction effect of the foreign currency assets ratio and exchange rate fluctuation rate was found to be significant. In the Step 4, the value of the entire R^2 indicates 0.1966.

Between 2003 and 2010, the foreign currency assets ratio affected the foreign exchange gain ratio, and the effect can be seen to become bigger depending on the exchange rate fluctuation. R^2, as shown in <Table 19>, can be seen as sharply increased in Step 4. It can be found that the foreign exchange gain ratio should consider the adjustment effect of the exchange rate fluctuation rate to the foreign currency assets ratio.

<**Table 19**> Result of stepwise panel analysis using the fixed effects model

Entire period (2003-2010)

Category	Step 1	Step 2	Step 3	Step 4
Constant	0.0019 (-2.13**)	0.0020 (-0.49)	0.0009 (-0.22)	-0.0016 (-0.46)
FAR	-0.0314 (-2.78***)	0.0342 (-2.39**)	0.0358 (2.51**)	0.0345 (2.75***)
EXP		-0.0130 (-1.73*)	-0.0112 (-1.50)	-0.0068 (-1.03)
FLR		0.0148 (-1.13)	0.0171 (1.32)	0.0236 (-2.06*)
DER		-0.1042 (-7.05***)	-0.1232 (-7.85***)	-0.0836 (-5.96***)
FXR			-0.0135 (-3.46***)	-0.0592 (-13.40***)
FAR*FXR				0.57 (-16.39***)
F value	7.72***	14.81***	14.39***	60.24***
R^2	0.0011	0.0249	0.0341	0.1966

Note. *Significant at p <.01. **Signigicant at p <.05. ***Significant p <.001.

Sub-period 1(2003-2006)

Category	Step 1	Step 2	Step 3	Step 4
Constant	0.0014 (-1.5)	0.0106 (-1.86)	0.0110 (-1.91*)	0.0052 (-0.88)
FAR	-0.0172 (-1.34)	-0.0109 (-0.53)	-0.0114 (-0.55)	0.0195 (-0.89)
EXP		-0.0241 (-2.32**)	-0.0235 (-2.25**)	-0.0184 (-1.78*)
FLR		0.0367 (-1.64)	0.0371 (-1.66*)	0.0423* (-1.93)
DER		0.5917 (-5.22***)	0.5998 (-5.24***)	0.6517 (-5.78***)
FXR			0.0098 (-0.53)	-0.0445 (-1.90*)
FAR*FXR				0.6488 (-3.64***)
F value	1.79***	8.81***	7.08***	8.38***
R^2	0.0557	0.0865	0.0894	0.1312

Note. *Significant at p <.01. **Signigicant at p <.05. ***Significant p <.001.

Sub-period 2(2007-2010)

Category	Step 1	Step 2	Step 3	Step 4
Constant	-0.0037 (-1.95)	0.0089 (-1.16)	0.0076 (-1.01)	0.0039 (-0.59)
FAR	0.0461 (-1.8)	0.0514 (-1.94*)	0.0558 (-2.13**)	0.0407 (-1.81*)
EXP		-0.0302 (-2.03**)	-0.0269 (-1.82*)	-0.0186 (-1.47)
FLR		-0.0005 (-0.02)	0.0023 (-0.1)	0.0147 (-0.77)
DER		-0.1118 (-6.20***)	-0.1348 (-7.09***)	-0.0972 (-5.88***)
FXR			-0.0164 (-3.48***)	-0.0595 (-11.42***)
FAR*FXR				0.5437 (-13.14***)
F value	3.24*	11.3***	11.53***	41.86***
R^2	0.0121	0.0326	0.0549	0.2726

Note. *Significant at p <.01. **Signigicant at p <.05. ***Significant p <.001.

3.4 Analysis on the interaction effects through two-way ANOVA

It is clear that the foreign exchange fluctuations on foreign currency assets makes the effect as moderating effect. Depending on foreign currency assets, foreign exchange gains can be explained by changes in accordance with the foreign exchange fluctuations. In order to confirm this interaction, this book conducted a two-way ANOVA. <Figure 39> shows the significant interaction clearly. Here this book classified foreign asset rate (FAR) with two categories. The foreign currency assets ratio of the target company was based on 4.6% against total assets. Foreign currency assets was classified as low from less than 4.5%, more than 4.6% was classified as high.

This classification is divided on the number of observation. This is for reviewing how the interaction appears to the independent variables with the controlled variable. Foreign exchange fluctuation rate (FXR) was divided into positive group and negative group. If the rate of the current year is increased from the rate of the previous year, it is classified as positive group. If the rate of the current year is decreased from the rate of the previous year, it is classified as negative group. <Table 14> shows all of the negative foreign exchange fluctuations in the first sub-period of four years. Relatively less exchange rate fluctuation was in 2003 (-1.2%) and 2005 (-2.5%). So, FXRs of the years are classified to positive group. The reason is that this is for showing only the interaction with foreign exchange fluctuation rate (FXR) and the foreign currency asset rate (FAR) through the two-way ANOVA. <Figure 39> clearly shows that the slopes are different from about two groups. In the entire period, the difference appears clearly between positive group and negative group. The positive group has less change than the negative group which has a significant change. The foreign exchange gain rate (FXG) is falling down very significantly on the high group of the foreign currency asset rate (FAR). Negative group is not different from the direction of the entire period and sub-period 1 and sub-period 2. But in the positive group, the direction is changed in the sub-period 1 and period 2 lower. The line is downward-sloping in the sub-period 1, and upward- sloping in the sub-period 2. The results are reasonable, because 2003 (-1.2%) and 2005 (-2.5%) are set to positive in the sub-period 1, even they are negative, actually. The foreign exchange gain rate is reduced in the sub-period 1. It means that the more foreign currency assets increase, the lesser the exchange gain decrease, because foreign exchange fluctuation rate is negative. However, the low foreign currency assets ratio make low foreign exchange gain in the positive group of the sub-period 2. And the high rate of foreign currency assets has a high foreign exchange profit. In particular, foreign exchange fluctuations in 2008 increased to 41% against the previous year. Through this, it seems no wonder of soaring foreign exchange gain. This book shows the foreign currency asset rate (FAR) as independent variable has the impact of the interaction through foreign exchange fluctuation rate (FXR) as the moderating variable, on the foreign exchange gain rate (FXG) as dependent variable.

<Figure 39> The results of two-way ANOVA during the period

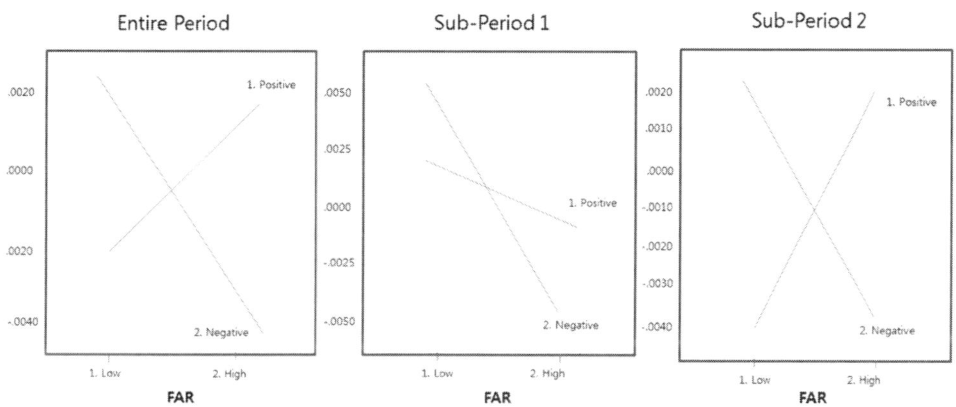

This method shows the interaciton effect to foreign exchange gain rate between foreign currency asset rate and foreign exchange rate. As a result, <Figure 39> supports for both hypotheses.

[Hypothesis 1] The foreign currency assets ratio during the period affected the foreign exchange gain ratio.

[Hypothesis 2] The foreign currency assets ratio would be moderated by the exchange rate fluctuation ratio in affecting the foreign exchange gain ratio during that period.

3.5 The moderating effect on system dynamics

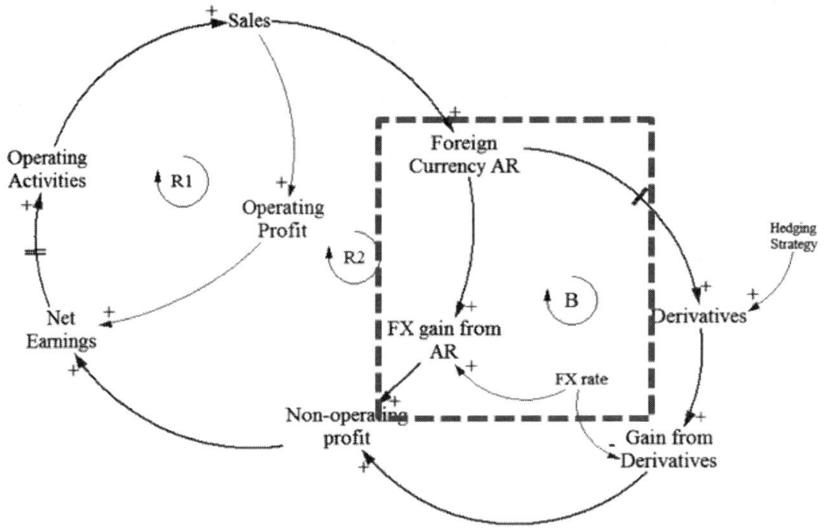

<Figure 40> The moderating effect of FX rate from <Figure 19>

Through a study of 3.4., it showed that <Figure 40> from the simulation on system dynamics supported the moderating effect. <Figure 19> explained that FX rate made effects to the foreign exchange profit, generated in accordance with the foreign currency receivables. The analysis of the system dynamics in the previous chapter had described. Exchange rate fluctuations have the effect on foreign currency receivables and derivatives. The paper has been limited to identifying some causal parts, even system dynamics reflects the causal factors and cyclical factors. <Figure 19> has been made in a number of causal relationship. Sales will affect the foreign currency receivables and foreign currency accounts receivable affects the foreign exchange gain or loss in accordance with the foreign exchange fluctuations. This affects the non-operating profit, which affects the income. Additionally, the income after tax has continued to invest in the company. Through this loop, the sales of the company is increased. Also, Companies purchase derivatives as financial purpose. So, they can manage the foreign exchange risk.

The system dynamics has different philosophy from empirical study. Many studies in the system dynamics has not used the empirical research. However, if a paper use both studies, it could be more valuable than only one. and system dynamics can be defended from the criticism as it has too assumption.

4. Implication and limitation of study

4.1 Implication of study

In this study, in order to analyze the effect of the foreign exchange currency assets for the foreign exchange gains, by targeting the period before and after the financial crisis, it is verified by using the panel data analysis. As the sample companies, it targeted 443 companies that have continuously, from 2003 to 2010, been listed on the Korea Stock Exchange, or registered in KOSDAQ, and it was eight years of 2003 to 2010. For the panel data, it structured the cross section unit of 443 individual companies, and it used the balanced panel data in which each company has a time series of eight years. If the existing studies on the exchange exposure have examined the change in the corporate values by the exchange rate fluctuation, this study has confirmed a direct impact of the corporate financial statements which become an indicator of corporate value. Bae & Jeong (2012) also studied on the accounting risk of exchange risk. However, there are not many studies that have attempted to financial analysis via panel analysis.

Companies, in response to the decrease in profits by the exchange rates fluctuations, buy derivatives. Although this does not have a big impact at ordinary time, in the time when the exchange rates fluctuation appears in big like the financial crisis, the derivatives play the role of hedge of exchange risk. However, such efforts of companies are not actually a big help. As it was confirmed before, the company, at ordinary times, seems not to be sensitive about the role of exchange rate hedge. Although using derivatives in matching the foreign currency assets and foreign liabilities that are increased or decreased by business activities, it is possible to confirm that it has not played the role of exchange hedge in the financial crisis. Companies seem to need in more practical to manage the correlation between the foreign currency assets and foreign exchange gains and losses in stable period of exchange rate.

Indeed, considering that fact that the amount of damage by KIKO in the period of the financial crisis reached 3 trillion and 200 billion (October 2010, Financial Supervisory Service), it is doubtful whether the function of derivatives had been performed properly. This seems that at a time when the exchange rate fluctuates in great, although the foreign currency assets have a significant impact on the exchange gains, the companies were not appropriate for the exchange hedge. Of course, when checking the correlation coefficient through the study earlier, it was confirmed that the function of derivatives has been performed to some extent in most companies. However, the registration of derivatives in which some companies enough to lead to bankruptcy is determined to have an adverse effect on the financial status of the company. This is a part that was also confirmed in the paper of Kim & Jun (2012).

This book examined the direct impact of exchange rate fluctuation on the corporate accounting value, and the indirect effects through the adjustment effect, too. In a situation that there are not many papers summarizing the impact of the exchange rate fluctuations on the corporate finance, this will be able to provide sufficient implication in that companies have to consider the impact of corporate finance in the exchange hedge.

4.2 Limitation of study

The materials used for this study was carried out through the financial statements data of companies that were extracted from FNGUIDE for the non-financial manufacturing companies out of the listed or registered companies. Although it could get the information of financial statements, the information such as the registered size of derivatives, income amount, and settlement currency of the companies could not be obtained. Since they are companies' information that is not disclosed, it is difficult to view. In addition, the study on the foreign currency liabilities also has not been carried out properly. If the exports had an impact on the foreign currency assets, the import or foreign currency borrowings affected the foreign exchange liabilities. However, it was not possible to get the significant values for this. Thereby, this study had no choice but to have limitations. For a more meaningful study, I hope the future analysis can be performed based on various data. If possible, I hope that the study be made in target of small and medium-sized companies not listed, and the paper can come out that can be used as a reference for even small and medium-sized companies to respond effectively to the exchange risk.

VI Overall Conclusion

This book is written for the management of exchange rate risk. It proceeds the literature review with system dynamics. It was published with the meaningful study which had analyzed the complicated structure on finance. And it tries the simulation of system dynamics with the derivatives related to exchange rate. It is very useful to study KIKO. The study on the view of what derivatives is active and dynamic. It was published separately on confirming what the simulation could be very proper study for financial market. Additionally, the empirical study shows the analysis of the causal relation of financial statements with statistical method. It supports the previous chapters on the base of system dynamics.

In this research, the comprehensive relationship between the exchange rate and the company's financial structure was studied through the causal loop diagram. This may give a reader to easily understand the complex impact from exchange rate. One could see that depending on the sales structure of a company, there may be changes in various relationships. Through this, one could take a look at the adequate foreign currency risk management strategy. In addition, this research developed the causal loop diagram into a stock-and-flow approach and tried simulation. In particular, it understood the problems that might occur in foreign currency risk and its hedging based on KIKO, a derivatives product. It showed that a company might suffer from a large foreign exchange loss because of wrong decision. Through system dynamics simulation, this book introduced an actual case and showed that companies might face a grave threat because of the fluctuation in exchange rate. Through this, it delivered a lesson that companies should carry out proper hedging, based on understanding of their financial structure. It explained the impact from exchange rate on corporate finance through secondary data.

There are three academic contributions in this study. The studies of the system dynamics for foreign exchange are still rare. The paper presented a model that can be expanded in the field of system dynamics. System dynamics has improved in various studies. It was also developed in the business area, such as learning organizations. However, there are not many attempts in the financial sector. This book was attempting significantly. Especially, the paper introduces the income statement with a causal structure of the system dynamics. It seems to be an enormous help in future studies of the relevant areas. Because it can easily shows the financial number of patterns with causal relationship. Second, the empirical studies are prime methods in the field of corporate finance. A variety of research methods were not being introduced to this field, compared to other business areas. Financial research has been recognized as an area that is difficult to introduce new areas of research. Through this book, the research method of system dynamics was an opportunity that can be useful in the financial area. A presentation of the various causal map was to be good method in the field. Also it is shown that the meaningful diagram which were introduced by the simulation of this book can be described in financial data. Third, this book showed sufficiently complementary role by complementing the statistical methodology with utilizing the system dynamics. Both areas often criticize each other with the different philosophy. While quantitative economists pursuit forecasting short-term accuracy, system dynamics researchers try to predict long term patterns. But through the methodology of statistical time series analysis, it shows how to explain well the results from system dynamics.

There are three practical contributions in this study. First, many companies handled out the exchange rate only as external influences. SMEs showed a passive response, rather than proactive response. This book presents a method for the risk management to access the structure of the company owns. Upon confirming the structure of the company well, it can be considered a suitable strategy. So, it could be helpful in foreign exchange risk management. It will be helpful to SMEs. Second, the causal maps and partial simulation presented in this book can be utilized in diagnostic research for financial statements. According to the company structure, the external influence may determine the impact of the financial numbers. In practice, it may be able to help to identify the effects related to the whole structure of the company. Third, The paper shows the possibility that looks at the financial impact of the other risk factors of an company. It showed the risk from the derivatives, identifying the failure of the strategy. This can be tested with other risk factors, like the sudden rise of oil price or the cost of manufacturing. If there are various simulations with the actual cases, it will be practically useful in the business fields.

If adequate measures are established and prepared, one may escape from the foreign currency risk. Even though the companies suffer from serious foreign currency risks every year, they have difficulties in coming up with the proper measures. In addition, some face serious threats due to dramatic fluctuation in the exchange rate. Since it lets the companies take a look at the foreign currency exposure structure and come up with the responses, it may help the companies escape from the risks. Companies may make themselves free from the potential threat from the foreign currency risk through implementing the strategy to alleviate the foreign currency exposure. The fluctuation in exchange rate may cause crisis to a company, but it may give a chance to beat the competition to those who have adequate strategy to alleviate the foreign currency exposure.

Since the lessons and limitations of the research have already been explained in detail in each chapter, the explanation on those will not be given again. However, it should be emphasized that through this research, it was shown that the system dynamics approach was very useful in understanding the impact of exchange rate to businesses. SMEs should have the view of system dynamics on the kind of issues. The exchange rate exposure could be managed.

■ References

Adler, M., & Dumas, B. (1984), Exposure to currency risk: definition and measurement. *Financial Management*, 13(2), 41-50.

Ban, H., & Kim, S (2006), Interaction effect of hedging strategy on Korean companies. *Korea Trade Review*, 31(3), 5-28

Bartram, S.M., Brown, G.W., & Minton, B.A. (2010), Resolving the exposure puzzle: The many facets of exchange rate exposure. *Journal of Financial Economics*, 95, 148-173.

Bertalanffy, L. (1976), *General System Theory*. George Braziller Inc.

Bian, A., Park, K., & Cho, J. (2006), Exchange rate exposure of Korean companies: Pre- and post- economic crisis analysis. *International Business Journal*, 17(3), 1-22.

Bodnar, G. M., & Wong, M. H. (2003), Estimating exchange rate exposure: Issues in model structure. *Financial Management*, 32, 35-67.

Bodnar, G., Hayt, G., & Marston, R. (1998), Wharton survey of derivative usage by US non-financial firms. *Financial Management*, 27, 70-92.

Breusch, T., & Pagan, A., R. (1980), The Lagrange Multiplier Test and its Application to Model Specification in Econometrics. *Review of Economic Studies*, 47, 239-253.

Cho, J., Bian, A., & Park, K. (2013), Currency crises and exchange rate exposure. *Korean Journal of Futures and Options*, 21(1), 49-70

Cho, S., & Song, M. (2011), Foreign exchange exposures of Korean firms during 2002~2009. *Journal of Korean Economic Analysis*, 17(2), 69-116.

Choi, C., & Ham, H. (2003), An analysis on the pass-through on Korean export prices of exchange rate changes. *International Commerce and Information Review*, 13(4), 229-249

Chung, C. (2001), Foreign exchange exposure management of the Korean automobile companies. *International Business Journal,* 12(1), 113-136.

Chung, C., & Lee, D. (2012), Exploratory study on causality of expansion strategy into emerging market: Systems thinking approach. *Korea System Dynamics Review,* 13(3), 67-98.

Chung, J., & Cho, H. (2011), Foreign exchange risk management by firm. *Review of International Money and Finance,* 1(2), 105-124.

Chung, T., & Lee, K. (2000), Foreign exchange risk management strategy of Korean firms. *International Business Journal.* 11(1), 57-86

Donella H. M., Dennis L. M, Jørgen R., & William W. B. (1972), *The Limits to Growth: A Report For the Club of Rome's Project on the Predicament of Mankind.* Universe Books. New York.

Donnelly, R., & Sheehy, E. (1996), The share price of u.k. exporters to exchange rate movements : An empirical study. *Journal of International Business Studies,* 1Q, 157-165.

Eom, J., Chung, C., & Sul, W. (2014), Exploratory study on causality of foreign exchange exposure and hedge strategy : Systems thinking approach. *Korea System Dynamics Review,* 15(2), 97-131.

Forrester. J. W. (1993), System Dynamics as an Organizing Framework for Pre-College Education. *System Dynamics Review,* 9(2), 183-194

George, S., & Grover, G. (1987), *The Alchemy of Finance: Reading the Mind of the Market,* Wiley Audio.

Gwag, T., Chung, C, Sin, S., & Choe, S. (2003), A *Study on the Foreign Exchange Exposure of Korean Exporting Companies. Journal of International Trade and Industry Studies,* 8(2), 135-153.

Hausman, J. A., (1978), Specification Tests in Econometrics. *Econometrica,* 46, 1251-1272.

Hong, Y., & Jung, S. (2007), Analysis on Research Trends of Korean System Dynamics : Results and Reflections of 7 years and Proposals. *Korea System Dynamics Review.* 8(1), 25-47.

Huh, Y., & Park, S. (2011), The effect of foreign exchange rate changes on firm performance forecast. *Korean Journal of Accounting Information,* 29(4), 301-330.

Jeong, S., Bae, S., & Lim, T. (2012), The association between foreign currency risk exposure and analysts` forecast properties. *Korean Accounting Review,* 37(4), 1-27.

Jeong, Y., & Chung, H. (2012), Foreign echange exposure of Korean firms and its relationship with foreign investors' investment, *Korean Management Review,* 41(6), 1285-1307.

John D. Sterman (2010), *Business Dynamics,* McGraw-Hill.

Jorion, P. (1990), The exchange-rate exposure of U.S. multinationals. *Journal of Business,* 63(3), 331-345.

Jung, J., & Kim, H. (2009), A study on theoretical improvement of casual mapping for dynamic analysis and design. *Korea System Dynamics Review.* 10(1), 33-60.

Jung, S., & Kwon, T., (2007), Does the use of foreign currency derivatives in Korean firms reduce the exchange rate exposure ?. *International Business Journal,* 18(4), 37-63.

Khoo, A. (1994), Estimation of foreign exchange exposure : an application to mining companies in australia. *Journal of International Money and Finance,* 13(3), 324-363.

Kim, D., & Hong, Y. (2005), A Study on the Government Regulation with Systems Thinking - Focus on the Medical Fee Regulation -. *Korea System Dynamics Review,* 6(2), 53-71

Kim, D., & Park, S. (2003), The relationship between foreign exchange risk of multinational corportationes and their ADR and underlying stock returns, *Journal of International Trade and Industry Studies,* 8(2), 201-219.

Kim, D., Kim, J., & Park, R. (2013), Hedging, liquidity constraints and investment. *Journal of the Aviation Management Society of Korea,* 11(1), 125-140.

Kim, D., Moon, T., & Kim, D. (1999), *System Dynamics.* Seoul: Daeyoung Munwhasa

Kim, G., & Jeon. J. (2001), Study of economic measurement and management on foreign exchange exposure for manufacturing companies. *International Business Journal,* 9, 69-99.

Kim, H. (2002a), Exchange rates and market power: alternative measure of residual demand. *The Korean Journal of Economic Studies,* 50(3), 307-340.

Kim, H. (2002b), The pricing-to-market effects of exchange rate with residual demand. *International Economic Journal,* 8(3), 63-93

Kim, J., & Ban, H. (2002), The determinants of hedging through derivatives. *Korean Management Review,* 31(5), 1335-1365.

Kim, S. (2008), *Systematic thinking and scenario planning.* Chungbuk National University Press

Kim, S. (2011), The effect of the interaction between FDI location and product differentiation on the foreign exchange exposure, *International Business Journal,* 22(2), 1-37.

Kim, S., & Jun, S. (2012), A case study on KIKO currency option. *Korea Business Review,* 16(1), 1-34.

Kim, S., & Kim, T. (2009), A study on the effectiveness of KIKO as a hedging instrument. *Productivity Review,* 23(4), 223-246.

Kim, Y. (2003), Effects on expected default risk of small-sized firms induced by drastic changes of foreign exchange rate during the Korea's financial crisis. *Korean Journal of Small Business Studies,* 25(4), 133-154.

Koh, S., & So, J. (2012), Foreign exchange risk hedge and firm value. *The Korean Journal of Financial Mangement,* 29(3), 23-54.

Kwak, T. (2004), Exchange rate pass-through and import prices in Korea`s manufacturing industries. *Journal of International Trade and Industry Studies,* 9(3), 1-25.

Kwon, O. (2012), Systems Thinking Approach to the Dynamic Relationship between Cash Market, Forward Market, and Options Market. *Korea System Dynamics Review,* 13(2), 5-23.

Kwak, T. (2012), International Economics : The effects of the exchange rate on investment. *International Area Studies Review,* 16(4), 161-184.

Kwon, T. (1998), The effect of currencies and asymmetry in estimating foreign currency exposure. *Korea Trade Review,* 23(2), 23-34.

Kwon, T. (1999a), The characteristics of the foreign currency exposure of the KOSPI 200 firms and non-KOSPI 200 firms. *Korean Management Review,* 27(5), 1311-1329.

Kwon, T. (1999b), An empirical study on the relationship between foreign exchange exposure and cost of financial distress - The case of Korean manufacturing companies - *International Business Journal,* 10(1), 177-197.

Kwon, T. (2001), Exchange rate change and markup adjustment of major Korean exports during Korea's foreign currency crisis. *Korean Management Review.* 20(2), 369-386.

Kwon, T. (2006a), Lagged exchange rate exposure and determinants of exchange rate exposure. *Korean Management Review,* 35(3), 735-756.

Kwon, T. (2006b), The exchange exposure and the maximum exchange loss in exchange risk analysis. *The Korean Journal of Financial Engineering,* 5(2), 45-62.

Kwon, T. (2007), Asymmetric exchange rate exposure and foreign currency denominated debt, *International Business Journal,* 18(1), 87-110.

Kwon, T. (2009), Internal transactions within business group and management of foreign exchange exposure. *International Business Journal,* 20(4), 79-103.

Kwon, H. (2012), Systems thinking approach to the dynamic relationship between cash market, forward market, and options market. *Korea System Dynamics Review,* 13(2) 5-23.

Kwon, T. (2013a), Foreign currency derivatives and foreign exchange rate exposure management of kosdaq firms, *Korean Journal of Futures and Options,* 21(2), 223-254.

Kwon, T. (2013b), Foreign currency denominated debt and firm value. *International Business Journal,* 24(3), 51-72.

Kwon, T., & Hwang, H. (1999a), Analysis of characteristics of mark-up adjustment from fx fluctuation on export industry in Korea, *Korea Trade Review,* 24(2), 141-161.

Kwon, T., & Hwang, H. (1999b), The characteristics of currency exposure in Korean manufacturing companies. *International Business Studies.* 9(2), 35-63.

Kwon, T., & Joo, K. (2002), Determinants of mark - up adjustment according to the exchange rate change in korea`s major exports. *International Business Journal,* 13(1), 67-94.

Kwon, T., & Joo, K. (2004), Foreign exchange exposure and risk management of firms in the Yosu national industrial complex. *International Business Journal,* 15(4), 31-61.

Kwon, T., & Joo, K. (2011), A study on the expected and observed exchange rate exposure of Korean firms. *International Business Journal.* 22(2), 39-70.

Kwon, T., & Joo, K. (2013), Change of characteristic on foreign exchange exposure and plan of exchange risk management. *International Business Review,* 17(1), 91-114.

Kwon, T., & Jung, S. (2010), The effect of corporate currency forward and futures trading on the asymmetric foreign exchange exposure. *International Business Review,* 14(3), 93-117.

Kwon, T., & Park, J. (1999), Relationship between foreign exchange risk premiums and firm characteristics in the Korean stock market. *The Korean Journal of Financial Mangement,* 16(1), 245-260.

Kwon, T., & Park, J. (2013), Derivatives hedging, earnings management, and foreign exchange exposure. *Korean Journal of Financial Studies* , 42(5), 865-899.

Kwon, T., & Park, R., & Chang, U. (2011), Effect of derivatives usage of Korean. *Korean Journal of Futures and Options.* 21(3), 331-351.

Kwon, T., Chang, U., & Jung, S. (2010), The usage of currency derivatives of the Korean firms and their management of the foreign exchange rate exposure. *The Korean Journal of Financial Management,* 27(4), 61-88.

Kwon, T., & Jung, S. (2010), Effects to asymmetric foreign exchange exposure from forward trading and currency forward trading. *International Business Review,* 14(3), 93-117.

Kwon, T., Park, R., & Bae, S. (2011a), Derivatives use, firm value, risk and determinants : evidence of Korean firms. *Korean Journal of Futures and Options,*

19(4), 335-362.

Kwon, T., Park, R., & Bae, S. (2011b), On the effectiveness of foreign exchange rate exposure hedging with derivatives for Korean industrial companies. *Korean Journal of Financial Studies,* 40(5), 829-861.

Lee, H. & Park, S. (2009), Foreign exchange exposure and its determinants of Korean listed companies. *Journal of Industrial Economics and Business,* 22(4), 1761-1781.

Lee, H. (1999), The Relationship between foreign exchange exposure and characteristic variables of the Korean firms and industries. *The Korean Journal of Financial Management,* 16(2), 383-404.

Lee, H. (2003), The Foreign exchange exposure and asymmetrics on individual firms. *The Korean Journal of Financial Mangement,* 20(1), 305-329.

Lee, H. (2004), An Analysis of the foreign exchange exposure and determinants. *The Korean Journal of Financial Mangement,* 21(2), 65-98.

Lee, K., & Lee, M. (2004), Exchange rate variability and pricing behavior of Korean firms: the markup response in industrial level. *Kukje Kyungje Yongu,* 10(1), 101-139.

Lee, S., & Choi, Y. (2011), The effects of foreign exchange volatility on export and firm's profit. *Journal of International Trade and Industry Studies,* 16(2), 57-78.

Lee, Y., Choe, J., & Kim, D. (2008), An economic analysis for effect of exchange rate fluctuation to corporate investment. *Journal of International Trade and Industry Studies,* 13(1), 203-222.

Miller, K. (1998), Economic exposure and integrated risk management, *Strategic Management Journal,* 19, 497-514.

Miller, K., & Reuer, J. (1998), Firm strategy and economic exposure to foreign exchange rate movements, *Journal of International Business Studies,* 29(3), 493-514.

Moore, J. F. (1993), "Predators and Prey : A New Ecology of Competition," *Harvard Business Review,* 71(3), 75-83.

Moore, T. (2007), *System Dyamics View on Sustainable City,* Jipmoondang.

Moon, T. (2012), System Dynamics View on Korea's Social Conflict and Policy Direction for Conflict Resolution, *Korea System Dynamics Review,* 13(1), 41-62.

Moon, T. & Seo, W, (2000), A study on the Waste management Policy Using System Dynamics Model, *Korea System Dynamics Review,* 1(2), 113-148.

Nam, G., & Xu, H. (2011), The foreign currency risk and firm value. *The Korean-Japanese Jounal of Economics and Management Studies,* 53, 139-166.

Oh, M. (2004), A practical study on the exchange risk management of shipping companies. *Journal of Shipping and Logistics,* 41, 1-17.

Paek, W., Lee, K., & Park, Y. (2001), The association between stock returns and performance measures: Comparison of relative information content among operating cash flows, net income, abnormal earnings, free cash flows, and economic value added. *Korean Academic Society of Accounting,* 26(2), 67-87.

Park, J., & Change, B. (2013), The Exchange rate and interest rate exposures of Korean corporations. *Journal of Economics Studies,* 31(2), 1-29.

Park, J., & Chung, J. (2006), A study of exporting SMEs's strategies against exchange rate volatility. *Journal of Industrial Economics and Business,* 19(4), 1355-1375.

Park, J., Kwon, T., & Lee, W. (2008), Foreign investors response to the foreign exchange rate risk in the Korean stock markets. *The Korean Journal of Finance Management,* 25(4), 53-78.

Park, S. (2001), Exchange rate volatoility and the Korean exports. *Journal of Korean Economic Analysis,* 7(3), 179-213.

Park, S., Kim, H., & Bahng, D. (2009), Netting and hedging effect on the exchange risk exposure of the Korean export firms. *International Business Journal,* 20(4), 1-28.

Richardson, G. P. (1991), *Feedback Through in Social Science and Systems Theory,* University of Pennsylvania Press, Philadelphia

Roh, J., Yun, W., & Kim, S. (1998), International hedging under concurrent risks of input / output prices and exchange rate : The case of Korean oil refinery. *Korean Journal of Futures and Options,* 6, 153-185.

Senge, P. M. (1990), *The Fifth Discipline: The art and Practice of Learning Organization,* New York : Doubleday Currency

Shin, S. (2003), The impact of capital market imperfections and exchange rate uncertainty on corporate investment. *Journal of Money & Finance,* 17(1), 83-112.

Song, H., & Han, S. (2010), Testing the valuation effect of foreign exchange risk insurance in Korea. *The Korean Journal of Financial Management,* 27(2), 63-84.

Song, M., & Cho, S. (2011), Foreign exchange exposures of Korean firms during 2002~2009. *Journal of Korean Economic Analysis,* 17(2), 69-116

Yi, C. (2001a), Analysis of determinants of hedge on foreign exchange exposure of companies from export and overseas investment. *Journal of Economics Studies.* 57-87.

Yi, C. (2001b), Measurement and hedging of foreign exchange risk of export and import. *Journal of International Trade and Industry Studies,* 6(2), 57-83

Yi, C. (2003), Foreign exchange exposure and hedging determinant of derivatives of international transaction firms. *Journal of Money & Finance* 8(1), 113-143.

Yi, C. (2004a), Estimation of exchange exposure of Korea's firms on dollar and yen, *Journal of International Trade and Industry Studies,* 9(2), 141-162.

Yi, C. (2004b), Foreign exchange exposure and hedging of trade and foreign direct investment firms in Busan area, *Journal of Economics Studies,* 22(1), 57-87.

Yu, S., & Hong, H. (2009), Foreign exchange exposure of Korean firms. *Journal of Industrial Economics and Business,* 22(4), 1659-1682.

Yun, C. (1998), A study on the exchange rate risk management using futures and options: centered on the relation between the role options and financial options. *Korea Trade Review,* 23(2), 35-53

Yun, C. (2003), A study on the effective method of exchange risk management using derivatives. *Korea Trade Review,* 28(1), 97-116.

E-Today, April 8th, 2014. The demage for KIKO.

Financial Supervisory Service. April 2nd, 2014. Press Release.

Financial Supervisory Service. October 1st, 2014. Press Release.

Korea Accounting Standard Board. November 27th, 2009. the Generally Accepted Accounting Principle 2.44

Korean Trade Association(2014), http://stat.kita.net/main.screen, Date of search, Dec.05.2014

▣ APPENDIX: Equations

(1) Sales=INTEG(Operating Activities), Initial Value 1,619

Units: 100 M won/year

(2) Operating Profit=Sales*Operating profit rate

Units: 100 M won/year

(3) Operating profit rate=0.034(Constant)

Units: rate

(4) Account Receivables=Sales*AR rate

Units: 100 M won

(5) AR rate=0.14(Constant)

Units: rate

(6) Foreign AR=INTEG(Account receivables/2), Initial Value 10

Units: 100 M won

(7) KIKO=(Foreign AR/10)*Confidence of Profit for KIKO

Units: 100 M won

(8) Confidence of Profit for KIKO=GET XLS DATA('data.xls' , 'data' , '1' , 'A3'), Data inputs.

Units: Dmnl

(9) FX gain from AR=(Foreign AR/10)*FX rate

Units: 100 M won/year

(10) FX rate=GET XLS DATA('data.xls' , 'data' , '1' , 'A2'), Data inputs. (Annual average rate)

Units: rate

(11) Evaluation of KIKO=KIKO*FX rate*-1

Units: 100 M won

(12) "Non-operating Profit"=Evaluation of KIKO+FX gain from AR

Units: 100 M won/year

(13) net income="Non-operating Profit"+Operating Profit

Units: 100 M won/year

(14) Operating Activities=net income*0.5

Units: Dmnl

The Strategy of FX Risk Management in International Trade

2015년 10월 7일 | 초판 인쇄
2015년 10월 12일 | 초판 발행

지 은 이 | 엄재근
발 행 인 | 김은중
발 행 처 | 서울경제경영출판사
북디자인 | (주)우일미디어디지텍

주 소 | 03767 서울특별시 서대문구 신촌로 205 대현빌딩 5층
전 화 | 02)313-2682
팩 스 | 02)313-8860

등 록 | 1998년 1월 22일 제5-63호

ISBN 978-89-97937-37-0 93320 정가 12,000원